CW01668202

EVIL EYE

The junkyard spaceship was going mad. The ion drive was cutting out. The starters, untriggered, kept cutting in, throwing the ship into convulsive spins.

'We've got to land,' Ispex yelled in Makenzi's ear. 'Land somewhere, anywhere!'

Shambles said, 'P-pardon. I have a landfall . . . this planet is sometimes called "Evil Eye" by human space travellers . . .'

'Terrific. Marvellous,' Vawn said – and was sick.

The Starstormers escape from the wicked Octopus Emperor only to find themselves in what seems a jungle filled with monstrous life forms – and watching eyes. What forces threaten them? How can they survive and escape?

This is the fourth story in the Starstormer Saga

Also by the same author,
and available in Knight Books:

The Starstormer Saga:
STARSTORMERS
SUNBURST
CATFANG

LEADFOOT

FLAMERS! (First published in
hardback under the title
ESCAPE FROM SPLATTERBANG)

Evil Eye

Nicholas Fisk

KNIGHT BOOKS
Hodder and Stoughton

Copyright © Nicholas Fisk 1982

First published by Knight Books 1982

British Library C.I.P.

Fisk, Nicholas
Evil eye.
I. Title
823'.914[J]   PZ7

ISBN 0 340 27076 4

The characters and situations in this book are entirely imaginary and bear no relation to any real person or actual happening

This book is sold subject to the condition that it shall not, by way of trade or otherwise, be lent, re-sold, hired out or otherwise circulated without the publisher's prior consent in any form of binding or cover other than that in which it is published and without a similar condition including this condition being imposed on the subsequent purchaser.

Printed and bound in Great Britain for Hodder and Stoughton Paperbacks, a division of Hodder and Stoughton Ltd., Mill Road, Dunton Green, Sevenoaks, Kent (Editorial Office: 47 Bedford Square, London, WC1 3DP) by Hunt Barnard Printing Ltd., Aylesbury, Bucks.

WHAT'S HAPPENED SO FAR

'Roses, strawberries and wine,' Makenzi's father, Jass, had said. 'We can grow them now, today, here on Epsilon Cool, millions of kilons from Earth. Just think of the future!' He smiled. The future looked good.

The present was very good. His son Makenzi was sound asleep, his adventures in the crazy, junkyard spaceship Starstormer *over at last. The other Starstormer children were safely sleeping too. Tsu, whose slanted dark eyes never showed fear; Vawn, often tearful yet possessed of strange strengths of her own; Ispex, who glared furiously through his old-fashioned, 20th-century spectacles and told the others, 'Think! Why won't you think!' Even Fang, the warrior cat, was asleep; and Shambles, the Starstormers' robot, had fallen into an electronic doze. So at last the Starstormers and their parents were together and at peace.*

But then the Voice of Tyrannopolis sounded. 'Obey!' it shouted. 'Obey the Octopus Emperor, the lord of Tyrannopolis! He demands your children! Surrender them, or . . .'

The threat was real and terrible. The strike power of Tyrannopolis was out there in space, ready and menacing. It could rend the fragile domes that held in the atmosphere of the human settlement – kill its occupants – or force them to flee into the unknown and infinite perils of space . . .

DESTRUCTION

The Voice of Tyrannopolis filled the speakers. There was no way of keeping the Voice out, no way of turning it off. It could seep into any place, the black dust that formed Tyrannopolis. Intelligent dust. Dust that could carry the commands of its ruler, the Octopus Emperor.

'Obey!' said the Voice. 'You do not obey!'

The Voice struck chill. Nobody could find an answer to it.

'What do you think he'll do?' whispered Vawn's mother, Sheila. 'Do you think he'll attack the settlement – the domes?' The question was not worth answering. Her voice petered out.

The Voice grated, 'Give us your children! Surrender the children! The Emperor has made his promise that they will be returned when they have borne children of their own. His word is law. Obey him and you may live at peace. Disobey, and . . .'

Ispex's father, Clyde, got up silently and left the room. He went to his sleeping son, knelt by him and shook his shoulder.

'Wake up, son! Wake up!'

Ispex looked blearily at his father and said, 'I was *asleep*.' He groaned and reached, as always, for his spectacles.

'I know. Listen, things are happening. Bad

things. The Voice threatens – well, you know.'

'I know. Threatens to rip up the settlement. Look, Dad, it's all right. We'll do what the Emperor wants. Turn ourselves in. It will be all right. It's not for ever. Just a few years.'

'No. We'd never let you sacrifice yourselves.'

'You can't not let us. I mean, *think*. What's the alternative? If we don't do what the Emperor wants, everyone's finished.'

'There is an alternative,' Clyde said. 'Escape! Escape in *Starstormer*!'

Makenzi was awake now. He said, 'What? And leave you here to face the Octopus Emperor? He'll tear the place apart and you'll all be dead!'

'He won't do that,' Clyde said, trying to sound sure of himself. 'We're no good to him dead. He needs human skills – our hands, our ability to handle tools. And even if he rips up the domes, we can still survive. Just lock ourselves in Control. Isolate ourselves. We've plenty of food and water and air –'

'*Plenty*?' Makenzi said. 'OK! Then why don't we stay with you? I mean, all that good food and water and air . . .?'

Clyde looked miserable and stayed silent. Ispex nodded at Makenzi and said, 'There's not enough of anything for even a few people. Certainly not enough for everyone. So we've got to obey the Emperor. Got to go.'

'Escape,' Clyde said, hollowly. 'Get into *Starstormer* and get out.'

'*Starstormer*'s a mess,' Makenzi said. 'Nothing works properly.'

More of the parents crowded into the little room. Jass, black and enormous, entered. 'You lot are getting out,' he said to Ispex and Makenzi. He grinned. His white teeth seemed to light up his dark face. 'You're getting into *Starstormer* and blasting off. That's my decision.' Suddenly all the arguments that had gone before seemed out of date. 'Get going,' Jass said to Makenzi.

Makenzi said, 'But –' and obeyed.

An hour later, the Starstormers blasted off into space. The parents watched them go. Now Jass's face was a lifeless black mask of misery. The other faces were grey. Meg cried silently in Sheila's arms. 'We had to make them go, didn't we?' Meg said. 'It was the only way. It was, wasn't it?'

Sheila could not answer. She stared into space, following the dwindling flares of *Starstormer*'s drives.

Then the light was gone.

*   *   *

Very soon, the missiles came. They screamed in, blattering and tearing at the outer atmosphere of Epsilon Cool, searing through it; they ripped through the transparent domes that protected the settlement.

Jass and Verona, Sheila and Dexter, Clyde and Meg stood on the roof of Control. They watched the destruction. Nobody spoke until Meg said, 'Shouldn't we take cover?' She spoke without particular interest. If one of the projectiles killed her, she would not mind. Her heart was in *Starstormer*.

'They're not aiming for us,' Clyde said. 'Just for the domes.'

'They don't want us dead,' Sheila said, bitterly. 'We might come in useful some day. The Octopus Emperor never *wastes* anything –' Another missile screamed and ripped. It flew flat, laying waste the domes, then hurtled on, not hitting the ground.

Verona said, 'Can't we put up some sort of fight?' She looked up at Jass, urging him with her eyes to exert some of his energy and strength. But his face was dead.

'Why waste what weapons we've got?' he said. 'We can't stop them. We can't even see the ship they're using.'

'I suppose we can mend the domes,' she said. 'Eventually –'

'And they can rip them apart again, any time they like,' Jass replied.

'Then why don't we just give in – quit Epsilon Cool – try to get home to Earth?' Verona said, knowing what answer she would get.

She got it. Jass's eyes came alive and blazed at her. 'It's *our* settlement,' he said. 'We made it. We'll never surrender.'

Verona, very quietly, replied, 'Good'. She smiled to herself.

Sheila shivered. She realised that there was a very slight draught, a gentle wind. She knew what it was: Epsilon Cool's atmosphere, rushing away from them, escaping into nothingness. Like the children.

'Soon we'll have to go inside,' she said. She thought, 'Soon, we won't be able to breathe. Soon, we'll have to lock ourselves into our own prison, the one safe place. And the TV eyes will show us all that we made crumbling to nothing. But the children are safe –'

'The children!' Verona said, suddenly and loudly. 'Why are we standing here? Why aren't we –' She ran indoors, into Control, and began scanning on the Navplan radio. Almost at once, she found voices.

'. . . Calling Epsilon Cool . . . come in . . .' It was Tsu speaking. 'We're OK, repeat OK, all OK. Come in, Epsilon Cool –'

'Tsu! Tsu! You're really OK? What's the state of the ship? Is ship OK? Over.'

The voice that replied was not Tsu's voice. It was the Voice of Tyrannopolis. It laughed. It said, 'Over, indeed! It's all over for you, my dear lady. You have disobeyed. The Emperor is displeased. The Emperor does not tolerate –'

Verona did not listen. Nor did the others. There was nothing to be said or done. All that remained was a hope, and a poor one at that – that *Starstormer* would hold together; that the children would find some sort of freedom, somehow, somewhere.

'Falling to pieces,' Ispex shouted. 'It's almost *funny*. It's almost a joke!' Behind his spectacles, his eyes were furious and also frightened.

The junkyard spaceship was going mad. The ion drive was cutting out. The starters, untriggered, kept cutting in, throwing the ship into convulsive spins.

'We've got to land,' Ispex yelled in Makenzi's ear. 'Land somewhere; anywhere!'

Shambles said, 'P-pardon. I have a landfall.' Luminous numbers and letters flowed over his sides. Ispex, dizzy and stumbling, tried to read them. 'What do they *mean*, Shambles? What's the *name* of the place?'

'B107D on the Galactic Grid,' Shambles said. 'Small planet. No name.'

'Not even a name,' Tsu said. Her head was spinning with the ship. 'Has it got a nickname?' she demanded.

'P-pardon? Nick? Nick?'

'Idiot! – oh lord, I can't stand upright! – a nickname, Shambles, a popular name, a –'

'Oh, I understand.' The robot's luminous readouts flickered and changed to a new pattern. Letters appeared and clustered into words on his sides. 'M-O-L-O-C-H.'

'Moloch!' said Vawn, miserably. 'Oh dear, oh

dear, I'm going to be sick – Moloch, what does that mean?'

'The D-devil,' said Shambles. 'Moloch is one of the names given to the King of Evil.'

'Great,' said Vawn. 'Great, just wonderful.' She tried to be sick into her bag but couldn't.

'Evil,' Shambles said. 'Yes, I have a reference for that word too. This planet is sometimes called "Evil Eye" by human space travellers. That is another nick-nick-*nickname*.' He sounded pleased with himself.

'Terrific. Marvellous,' Vawn said – and was sick.

'We've got to land on it all the same,' Ispex said. 'Even the Navplan's gone haywire –'

'We'll land,' Makenzi said. 'Get ready. Quick. Go to the Padded Cell and get strapped in.'

The Starstormers began to obey. The ship bellowed and belched. Shambles scurried and toppled as he tried to control the Navplan and bring the power units under some sort of control. A TV screen flickered and flared – then suddenly, for no reason, decided to give a picture of their new home.

It looked enormous. It filled the TV screen with untidy, luminous flaring images. 'It's big, very big,' Vawn said.

'Doesn't mean a thing,' Makenzi said. 'I mean, a *hotel* would fill the screens, we can't *judge* the size.'

'It's close!' Ispex yelled. 'We're too close! Get strapped in! –'

'Too late,' Makenzi said. 'Just hang on to something and pray.'

Starstormer hit.

The first contact was a sideways, glancing swipe. *Starstormer* crashed, shuddered, screamed and was suddenly in space again. But not for long. The gravity of the body she had hit sucked the little craft back. At the second impact, *Starstormer* began to cartwheel.

'Hold on!' Makenzi yelled, too late. All at once, the Starstormers were like dolls in a washing-machine, helpless dolls that tumbled and adopted grotesque positions, dolls that could be broken . . .

The noise of the impact changed. There was a vicious, bone-shattering jar; then a grinding slide against something solid. The grinding became a grating scream as the hurtling craft tried to burrow its way into whatever it had hit.

The scream died. Now there was only a rubbing noise, an untidy grating and clattering. It reminded Makenzi of films he had seen of twentieth-century underground trains coming into their stations. The noise started like that, then became lower as the train slowed . . .

Starstormer had stopped.

There was no noise any more, no movement. Only silence and stillness.

Tsu broke the silence. 'Nice landing,' she said, sweetly and sarcastically, in her high, clear voice.

Vawn said, 'Where's Fang?' She started looking about her, dazed but determined. She seemed unaware of the blood trickling down her arm from the elbow, which poked bloodily through a tear in her suit. 'Poor darling Fang,' she said. 'Where are you?'

Fang must have heard. He said 'Miaoww!', on a note of rising fury, and poked his indignant head out from under the console. He glared furiously at the Starstormers.

Makenzi began to laugh and could not stop.

Shambles flashed lights. 'P-pardon,' he said. 'But has anyone any instructions?'

'Mend Vawn's elbow,' Makenzi said, through his laughter.

Shambles obeyed. As he dabbed and patched, he said, 'B-but, pardon . . . The position could be serious.'

'What position?' Tsu said, icily. 'Do tell.'

Ispex began fiddling with the outside TVs. One of them worked. It gave an astonishing picture.

Most of *Starstormer* was buried. Only a third of the ship's body showed. Two-thirds was sunken in the powdery exterior of the thing they had hit.

'Like a bullet embedded in a brick,' Ispex said. 'At least we ended up right way up.'

He looked through an RV window and tried the exterior lights. Two lit: one immediately blew. The Starstormers caught a glimpse of smooth darkness: a regularly shaped darkness. Then the other lamp blew.

'Do you realise,' Tsu said, 'that our docking port faces inwards? We've landed so that we can open our lock-and-dock and walk straight into whatever it is that we've hit?'

'*If* we can get the door open,' Makenzi said. He was no longer laughing.

Vawn said, 'Why don't we just try the stupid door and find out?' Before anyone could stop her, she'd operated the lock-and-dock controls – the inner door swung open – the airlock hissed – and the outer door graunched and squealed and scraped, thrusting aside whatever it was that opposed it . . .

And *Starstormer* was suddenly filled with the warm stench of rotting vegetation.

'There you are,' Vawn said, smugly. 'The door's open. Anyone coming?'

And without a backward glance, helmetless, she walked through the door and into a wonderful, welcoming new world – certain death – anything at all.

THE JUNGLE

'It's a jungle,' Ispex murmured. 'Are you sure we don't need helmets, Shambles?'

The Starstormers had penetrated only a little way into their new world. They were framed in stalks and stems and leaves. Some of the leaves dripped. The air was hot and thick.

'You need helmets for physical protection against accidents,' Shambles told Ispex.

Ispex said, 'Hm. I wonder. Getting out of the ship and into this was sheer stu-pi-di-ty.' He glared spitefully at Vawn.

'I don't know what you're talking about,' she said, airily. 'I mean, we're here, aren't we? Still alive. Still breathing. And we can always go back.' She tried to throw back her wings of hair. But the hair caught against dripping leaves, strange leaves that brushed her face with clammy wetness.

'What do we do?' Makenzi said. 'I vote we get knives and things and go on. What do you say?'

'Got no choice,' Ispex said. 'So many things we need, for ourselves and for *Starstormer*. Might find them here, you never know.'

'Of course we'll go on,' Vawn said, trying to keep her voice calm. The wet ends of her hair felt horrible against her neck.

Tsu said, without emotion, 'We're being watched.'

'How do you know?' Makenzi demanded.

'Because I know. Wait for me.' She went back into *Starstormer* and soon returned carrying kitchen knives, choppers, anything that could cut and slash. 'One for you, and one for you and one for you,' she said. 'And rations for everyone in this sack. You carry it, Makenzi, you're the strongest. I'll carry the water. Vawn – sleeping bags. Ispex – weapons. I've anchored *Starstormer* and closed everything down.'

'Bossy as usual,' Vawn said, under her breath.

'Right as usual,' Makenzi told her.

They shouldered their burdens and began cutting and hacking at the jungle greenery.

In the first half hour, they made perhaps five hundred metres. Perhaps less. Then suddenly the way ahead became clear. The greenery had a big tunnel through it: a roughly circular tunnel that curved. They stopped, drank water and stared into the dim greenness.

'Want to go on?' Mak said.

'Yes,' said Vawn and Tsu.

'Yes,' Ispex said. 'But we'll leave a marker. This bleeper will do.' He stuck a bleeper into the pulpy earth (if it was earth). 'Everyone getting a signal? Yes? And you, Shambles?'

'Yes.'

'OK. Remember, if you have to, turn right at this bleeper, then tune to *Starstormer*'s bleep for the last leg home. OK?'

'Right.'

'OK.'

Pleased with his own efficiency, Ispex characteristically stuck out his lower lip, poked his spectacles firmly on to the bridge of his round nose and marched stoutly forward . . .

And fell flat on his face.

Something quick, long, glistening, pale and snake-like had wriggled through the undergrowth, its body snaking in a series of esses. One of the esses tripped Ispex.

'Did you see it?' he said, hollowly, as he gathered himself together. 'But you *must* have seen it! It was – it was *re-pul-sive* –' The white of his face was paler than ever.

'I saw a movement, just a movement,' Vawn said. 'But then, I keep thinking I see things move –' Her face began to hide itself behind her wings of hair.

'I told you,' Tsu said. 'We're being watched. Must be the Evil Eye.' No one disagreed. Her dark eyes slid from side to side under the slanted eyelids and her little white teeth bit her lower lip. Makenzi's eyes, too, were wide and uneasy and busily scanning. His right hand gripped a kitchen chopper – gripped it hard: black skin shone over the tense bones of his hand.

He said, 'Use your eyes, you lot. Look hard.'

They stood rigid and silent, looking. A strangely shaped leaf quivered when a drop of water fell on it; a coiled tendril of stem fell free. Everything dripped or was about to drip. 'A jungle,' Ispex muttered to himself. 'How? Why?'

Out loud, he said, 'This place is in-com-pre-hensible. I mean, it's Earthstyle, but it's not properly Earthstyle. These leaves and things, they're not right –'

Makenzi said, 'Sick-looking. Everything seems to be trying to wrap itself round everything else, sort of strangling. What's the matter, Vawn?'

Vawn was trembling. She said, 'Tsu's right. We're being *looked at*.'

There was a wet *plop*! and something fell from the top of a tall, twisted growth of thick-stemmed creepers. The thing that fell was like a jellyfish, almost. It was wet and green and soft. Its body was ridged like a peeled orange. The skirt was frilled and pinkish.

It fell, and covered something dark. Then quietly and wetly, it began to heave.

Under the frilled skirt of the thing, something stuck out, moving frantically. It looked like the tail of an animal.

The thing heaved and sucked and the tail – it was dark brown and made in hard, shell-like segments – began to disappear into the jellyfish skirt. It was drawn in with little jerks.

The tail stopped moving.

Vawn whimpered, 'Oh! . . . Oh! . . .'

Tsu pinched her arm. 'Shut *up*!' she said, in her metallic voice. 'Keep still!'

The tail of the animal was hidden. Ispex tried to make his brain work. The jellyfish must be about half a metre across, therefore the animal it was eating would be less than half a metre, therefore –

'Look!' said Makenzi's urgent voice in his ear. 'By the jellyfish!'

Ispex looked and saw dark snouts and red eyes. The eyes seemed to have no pupils – to be simply red marbles. The snouts wrinkled and curved fangs showed. Ispex thought of bats.

Now all of the creatures – there were five – were in the open and creeping closer to the jellyfish. Vawn saw their bodies and whimpered again. The heads were rat-like, the ears raw and huge. The upper ridge of.the humped bodies was scaled and the scales tapered along the length of the sharply pointed tails.

One of them jumped. The jump was instantaneous. There seemed to be no time – no gap between the animal being on the ground and flying through the air, spinning as it flew. Back arched, it landed tail first on the jellyfish. The pointed, scaled barb of the tail went straight into the green jelly. The jelly shrank, puckered and leaked a thick, clear fluid.

The other four creatures imitated the first. They sprang upwards, turning as they flew so that their tails lanced the jellyfish. The jellyfish began to collapse, shuddering and twitching. The five creatures darted at it, fangs bared. They cringed and darted, cringed and darted, tearing morsels from the pinkish skirt, gobbling them, choking them down.

The jellyfish twisted part of itself into a strange shape, as if it would turn itself inside out. It squirted shining liquid at one of its attackers. The jet of liquid splattered the attacker's face. The creature screamed then ran with insane energy into the undergrowth, squeaking, somersaulting, tripping, scrabbling at its eyes with its front paws.

And then Vawn was running, just as blindly –

running away and crying out as she ran.

They caught up with her. She was on her knees, weeping hopelessly. 'I want to get back to *Starstormer*,' she said. 'I want to get back to Fang.'

* * *

Safe home inside *Starstormer*, Vawn gradually recovered. Fang cured her. She buried her nose in the little cat's neck and breathed sanity and security from his warm furry body.

The others talked. Makenzi said, 'Like it or not, we've got to go out again. It looks sort of Earthstyle out there and we've got to have Earthstyle bits and pieces for the ship. We're stuck here without them. Shambles, you tell them.'

Shambles obediently displayed read-outs and recited lists of essential supplies.

Ispex ticked the items off on his fingers and scowled.

Tsu said, 'Weapons. I'm going to get weapons.'

'P-pardon,' Shambles said, when she had gone, 'But as I was saying – The liquids we encountered outside can be made drinkable and the vegetation is not p-poisonous and can therefore be cooked and the atmosphere is breathable and –'

Only Ispex listened. Makenzi scratched himself irritably and thought about weapons. Most of the ship's weapons, he knew, were too powerful. You can't blow holes in a strange planet because you don't know what evils may come out at you from the holes. You don't know what you may stir up. So the weapons had to be short-range and not too lethal. What did they have? They had some Stuns that sometimes worked . . .

Tsu came back with weapons. 'Stuns,' she said, throwing down small, crude gaspipe things with the paint chipped on their barrels. 'One each and one over. I bet they don't work properly –'

'Junk,' Ispex said miserably, looking up from Shambles. 'Junk and leftovers. What else, Tsu?'

'Burners,' Tsu said, handing him another battered gaspipe affair, longer and more complicated than the Stuns. 'Ispex, you can check these for us, can't you? Get them fully charged and everything? Then I'll test them into the ground. See whether they'll burn *leaves* or anything.' She rolled her eyes and shrugged.

Ispex said, 'My father says Burners don't give much trouble. I mean, they're not cartridge weapons, like Stuns. With Stuns, you get dud cartridges. But if a Burner works, it's likely to keep on working. Providing it will hold its charge . . .' He handled the Burner gloomily and looked along its sights. It had sights because it shot a laser-like beam. It was a very precise weapon. Or had been when it was new.

'We've also got the heavy stuff,' Tsu said.

'Oh no we haven't,' Makenzi said. 'No heavy stuff, *if* you please. Not until some sort of war breaks out or we have to get out in a hurry. Stuns, Burners, knives, spears, ordinary hand guns, anything you like – but no heavy stuff. And Ispex, don't point that Burner at me.'

Tsu, remembering all the experience Makenzi's parents had of alien places, did not argue. She said,

'All right then. You know best. Just the small stuff. I'm hungry. Let's eat.'

* * *

Vawn could not eat. She hid her face behind her hair so that only her nose stuck out. Occasionally a tear rolled down her nose and dripped on to her uneaten food. 'She's off,' Ispex whispered. 'One of her Big Glooms –'

Tsu, often looking sidelong at Vawn, ate greedily. 'Oh, *yummy*,' Tsu said, with an edge to her voice. 'Such dee-*lic*ious goodies. Try some, Vawn. Give you strength.'

Ispex nudged her, trying to make her stop. She wouldn't. 'We all need strength, Vawn,' Tsu continued. 'Strong little bodies, strong little minds. So if we eat all our good food and stop drizzling –'

Makenzi said, 'Cut it out Tsu.'

But Tsu took no notice. 'Eat it all *up*, there's a brave Vawny-pawny,' she said.

Vawn stood up; emptied her plate of soup over Tsu's head; and walked out.

'You asked for it,' Makenzi told Tsu. 'Being superior –'

'Soup,' Ispex said. His face went pink with pleasure because he was about to make a joke. 'Soup is what you get for being so *soup-erior*.'

Tsu, teeth bared, tried to get at Ispex. Makenzi held them apart. He was laughing now, the whole thing was so childish and ridiculous . . .

Then the three of them heard it: the unmistakable sounds the airlock made, the wheezings and hissings and dull clunks as the inner door opened, then the outer door . . .

'Vawn! She's leaving the ship!' Makenzi gasped. 'Stop her!'

They ran, frantically, and were too late. Vawn was gone. The doors were still wheezing and hissing as they laboriously closed and sealed themselves. It would take whole minutes for the closing cycle to be finished and the opening cycle completed.

'Come on, come on!' Makenzi urged the doors.

'It's already too late,' Ispex muttered. 'She could be anywhere by now. Stupid, stupid . . .'

VAWN, ALONE

Vawn sobbed as she stumbled along, 'Had enough,' she said to herself, through her tears. 'Enough of the whole rotten beastly thing. Better dead.' Automatically, her fingers adjusted her helmet and suit. She had put them on by habit. Or perhaps to keep the watching eyes, the evil eyes, of the jungle at a distance.

'Better dead!' she repeated, liking the words. Around her, little hidden things darted, scrambled, flew. Big things dripped, writhed, and relentlessly grew. A jellyfish creature, twenty metres above her, slithered and tilted, readying itself to drop on her. Vawn saw nothing. The jellyfish thing drew itself back and waited for another target. Vawn blundered on. Soon, she realised, she would have to stop to sort out the problem of blowing her nose with her helmet on. For the moment, she sniffed and wept and sniffed again.

She happened on a clearing of sorts – a place where a huge cluster of tree-like growths and creepers had died, rotted and collapsed on itself. She cleared a seat of tangled dead growths and sat on it. She twisted her helmet sideways and let her suit deliver tissues into her hand. She would blow her nose, replace her helmet, lie back and let whatever was going to happen, happen.

'Better dead,' she said, loudly. She had always been the odd one out. The other Starstormers didn't feel things as she did. They looked down on her because she had more imagination. Evil Eye . . . she could feel, almost touch, the evil. The others didn't understand the things she understood. She was sick of them, sick of *Starstormer*, sick of it all. A lazy contentment began to invade her.

She blew her nose and threw the tissues behind her. She did not replace her helmet – what was the point? They would find her skeleton, if they found anything of her at all, which was unlikely. Her eyes, focussed on nothing, saw a blur of green. She leaned back on her elbows and let the green take over her mind.

Behind her, unseen, the paper tissues moved.

They twitched and shifted in little jerks. Tiny noises were made by little teeth tearing at the paper fibres – by little paws pulling at them. Vawn did not hear.

Beneath her, there were slitherings and slidings as snake-like hunters made their silent way towards the owners of the paws and teeth. Vawn felt nothing. 'Had enough,' she said.

But suddenly she was bolt upright, all her senses alive. Eyes! She could feel them on her! Eyes everywhere, all staring at her! The eyes seemed to fire rays at her, beams that crossed in her mind, beams that burned. She stood up, breathing fast. She turned and turned, terrified, looking for the eyes.

She saw the tissues. As she stared at them, one of them turned over, jerkily, and was drawn downwards into the lattice of dead stalks. She gave a strangled scream.

A small, furry head popped up and looked at her with brilliant black-bead eyes. The body behind the head busily scuffled and raised itself on its hind legs.

Vawn and the animal stared at each other, motionless. Then a message, as clear as if it had been spoken in words, came from the animal and entered Vawn's mind. 'Can I eat you?' was the message.

'Of course you can't,' Vawn's mind replied. 'You're only a fieldmouse! Come here and let me look at you!'

SEARCH PARTY

'Check your weapons,' Makenzi said. He fired his own Burner into the ground. A black, burning hole appeared. Little flames leapt and died. Smoke curled. 'OK,' he said. 'And yours, Tsu? Yours, Ispex?'

'OK.'

'OK.'

'We'll take the Stuns on trust,' Makenzi said. 'No point in wasting cartridges. All right, let's move.'

They moved into the jungle. Very soon, *Starstormer* was hidden from them. They carried kitchen knives and choppers, improvised spears, Stuns and Burners. Ispex was draped with ropes, Tsu with food and water packs. Makenzi, when he had to, carried the heaviest burden, Shambles. The robot might come in useful. Anything might come in useful.

'Tracks,' said Ispex, pointing down at soggy earth. 'Shambles, can you see? Vawn's footsteps. Try your thermo, see if there's any warmth in them.'

'No thermo reading,' said the robot.

'Oh well, it was an idea,' Ispex said. 'We'll have to use our eyes –'

They found tracks and followed them. Makenzi was best. He seemed to have an instinct for picking up the trail when it had been lost in harder ground. Ispex was not so good. His mind was too logical. 'Don't know how you do it,' he said. Makenzi explained. 'She wouldn't walk in a straight line, she'd just wander on –'

Then he screamed. From a dim green nowhere, a creature hurtled at him and wrapped its six legs round his upper body and helmet. He pulled at the jointed legs and felt them crack and give but the heavy body, as big and hairy as a dog's, was still furiously active and the mouth was biting, sharp yellow teeth snapping at the helmet, trying to get at his face . . .

Tsu put the muzzle of her Burner right against the body: gritted her teeth: and drilled a white-hot hole through the spine of the creature. It arched its back, gaped its jaws and fell, still moving, at Makenzi's feet. He stumbled backwards and fell into a sitting position. When he could speak, he said, 'Supposing you'd burned through my helmet –'

'But I didn't,' said Tsu. Her sharp voice had a crack in it and her golden face a greenish tinge.

The creature twitched a last time and stopped moving. They examined it. It was hideous: and all the worse for being somehow familiar.

'Six limbs,' Tsu said. 'Four of them proper limbs and the front two stunted, like an afterthought. And very big jaws and teeth. Look at the tail! Like a monkey's. But the arms and legs aren't like anything on Earth –'

'P-pardon,' Shambles said. 'Earthstyle birds have bones of that sort.'

'It's not a bird, you moron,' Makenzi said, shuddering as he remembered the weight of the hairy body. 'It could be anything.'

'P-pardon, not an anything. It is a manythings. Many Earthstyle things, I do not understand.'

'It's mostly a mammal, by the look of it,' Tsu said.

'If it is a mammal, it will be warm-blooded,' Ispex said. 'Still be warm. Feel its body, Tsu.'

'You feel it. Or Makenzi.'

'Not me.' He poked his foot at the body. 'You, Shambles.'

Shambles extended a silvery whip and probed its point into the creature. 'Warm-blooded,' he said. 'Warm as in Earthstyle cat, dog, rabbit.'

'Ghastly thing,' Makenzi said. 'Mutant mess.'

'*Mutant* . . .?' said Ispex. 'Now, there's a thought . . .'

Vawn's feet were surrounded by fieldmice now. They were not at all afraid of her. They looked up at her with beady eyes, quivered their whiskers, tried to eat the soles of her boots. When she picked one up, it struggled uneasily and sent a message to Vawn's brain: 'I belong on the ground. It is bad up here.' So she put it down.

'I always knew I understood animals,' Vawn thought. 'I always knew I was sort of in touch with them. No one ever believed me.'

To the mice, she said, 'Is it nice living here?' No reply. Well, it was a stupid question, perhaps. Do mice know they're alive? Do they know of their own deaths? Or of good and evil? Of course not. She tried a more sensible question. 'Do you have enemies?'

She should not have asked. The mice jumped as if she had hit them – squeaked – looked about them frantically – and suddenly they were gone, all of them.

'You've got enemies,' Vawn said. 'Lots of enemies.'

She stared at the mass of vegetation into which the mice had disappeared; stared until the mass became a grey, brown and green haze. 'Talk to me, planet,' she murmured, 'if you are a planet. Tell me things –'

Nothing happened at first. Then, after a long time, she thought she heard a sort of musical wind blowing. The wind stirred no leaves, caused no branches to sway. It moved only in her head, rising and falling, a kind of music.

Now the music was talking. '*Hear usss*,' it seemed to say. '*Lisssten* –'

'I'm listening. Who are you? What are you? Are you the voice of Tyrannopolis?' She was thinking of their enemy, the tyrant planet, the world of dust, the home of the Octopus Emperor. Remembering them, she was afraid.

'*Not Tyrannopolisss*,' sang the music. '*Absssurd*!'

The music laughed and Vawn knew that it spoke the truth. The voice of Tyrannopolis never laughed except in scorn: and this was gentle music, kindly laughter.

'You sound nice,' Vawn said, 'but your planet is horrible! I hate it here on Moloch! Horrible creatures, everything killing everything else, everything rotting and rotten. I hate your planet!'

'*Not oursss*,' the voice replied. Then the music swelled. '*Yours! Yours! YOURS!*'

Vawn rose to her feet, startled. 'What do you mean, *ours*?' she said, loudly: so loudly that the music stopped and she was alone again.

Tsu, Ispex and Makenzi went on into the jungle, following Vawn's tracks. It was amazing how fast they learned the tracking game. They learned to look for footprints in the damp greenery, broken creepers. They used a new sort of commonsense – 'She wouldn't have got through that lot, so she must have gone through there –'

And they used Shambles. Once Tsu and Ispex had fiddled with him, tuned up his sensors, he learned to smell Vawn – or rather parts of her suit. 'C-cellulose acetate!' he said, happily waving a flexible probe. He became so enthusiastic that he did not have to be carried much. His wheels did not work on the soft ground, but his pads did. He shuffled and butted his way ahead until he got bogged down. 'P-pardon!' he said, still trying to refuse help but becoming more and more mired down. 'P-pardon, I need no assis-sis-sis-tance . . .' Not daring to laugh, Makenzi had to wait until even Shambles admitted defeat. Then he would pick up the robot and carry him.

Perhaps it was Shambles' attempt to be a Red Indian tracker that cheered the party. They were pretty sure now of finding Vawn. The shock of discovering and killing the strange animal had worn off. Makenzi said, 'Couldn't take the old Burner, could he? Really burned him up! Right through him, *zizz*! Fried pork!' He waved his spear, aimed the Burner at nothing in particular and did a little war dance.

Tsu said 'Don't be stupid!' and continued to look about her. Yet Ispex saw a sort of greediness in her look, as if she wanted to find another creature: and noticed her slim finger caressing the trigger. Sometimes she licked her lips.

He was just starting to say, 'Those big creepers, you'd think they were moving about,' when one of the creepers flung itself at him like the thong of a whip and caught his ankle. He yelled and other creepers lashed at him, writhing and encircling his legs and body. The tips of the creepers widened and flattened into spoon shapes and in the centre of each spoon there were thorns round a little soft, pale hole like a mouth. Ispex yelled: then, as the creepers multiplied and tightened round him and he was pulled to the ground, he began screaming, strange screams that did not sound like any noise that Ispex could make.

Tsu was even quicker than Makenzi in coming to his rescue. With her left hand she pointed her Burner at the roots of the creepers: with her right, she slashed at creepers with a meat axe. Then Makenzi was in action too, sweeping his Burner across the angle of creepers, lashing and slashing at the stems . . .

Suddenly he stopped and ran away. Tsu screamed 'Mak! You! – you! –' But he stood with his back to her, his shoulders high and hunched and his legs braced apart, blazing his Burner at targets she could not see. 'Coward!' she shouted.

'Help me! You coward!' But he left her to free Ispex.

Ispex sat up when the creepers were all destroyed and said, 'I'm all right. Per-fect-ly recovered.' He was shaking so violently that his helmet wobbled. Tsu wanted to inspect his suit for damage, but first the coward Makenzi had to be dealt with. She hit his shoulder with a chop that knocked him off balance and said, 'You great creep, I'd like to –' She spun on her heel and smashed him in the chest with a back kick that sent him sprawling.

He looked up at her with eyes whose whites looked huge in his black face. 'Cool it, Tsu!' he said. 'Didn't you see them? You must have! –' but she was coming at him again, slim hands like rigid blades ready to strike. He scrambled away from her and kept her at a distance with a spear. 'Stop it, you lunatic!' he shouted, half laughing and half angry. 'I don't want to fight you! You win, you win, OK? Just like Earthside, back at school! You *win*!'

Her hands relaxed. Makenzi got to his feet. 'Ispex OK?'

'Never mind Ispex. You really are scum, Makenzi, you really –'

'Shut up and come with me.'

She obeyed and followed him to the place where he had stood using the Burner. 'There,' he said. 'There, there and there. Take a good long look.'

She saw dead creatures. Creatures with tusks, creatures with fangs, furred creatures, nakedly raw creatures; creatures that were rag-bag assemblies of snakes and wild pigs, jackals and birds; creatures with the bodies of dogs and horny beaks like toucans; creatures with eyes that seemed blind, or great eyes glazed, dimming in death.

'It's mad,' she said at last. 'I'm mad, they're mad –'

'Nine of them,' Makenzi said. 'They were all coming to get Ispex. The creepers trap things and then this lot sort of battens on – goes in like jackals to get what's left. Like jackals and hyenas and vultures.'

'But we've never seen anything like them,' Tsu said.

'Well, we wouldn't. They wouldn't appear until dinner is served. Ispex was their dinner so out they came. Are you really all right, Ispex?'

'I've told you, I'm perfectly all right. I'm not a baby.' He was still shaking uncontrollably.

Tsu said, 'Check his suit, Shambles.' Under her breath, she told the robot, 'Check *him*, too.'

'How many *didn't* you kill?' Tsu asked Makenzi.

'I don't know. There seemed to be eyes everywhere. Up in the creepers, down in the undergrowth, everywhere. This place is a – freak zoo. Everything you can think of –'

'And everything you can't think of, don't want to think of,' she said. 'But how? Why?'

'Haven't a clue.'

'I think I have,' said a third voice. And Vawn was there.

'But we went out to find you!' Makenzi said, astonished.

'Well, I found you instead,' Vawn replied. 'You

were making enough noise with the Burners and everything. Who screamed?'

'Ispex. The creepers got him, and then all these mad animals –'

'I did not scream,' Ispex said. 'I merely shouted for assistance.' He looked better. 'What do you mean, you think you've got a clue, Vawn?'

'Well, it's not much of a clue, but it's a beginning. I had a sort of talk –'

'We're all going to have a talk,' Makenzi said. 'Back to the ship, for a Council of War.'

'And the voice told me that this planet is Earth-style. The life on it, I mean. The voice said, "This planet is *yours*".'

'Ah,' said Tsu, coldly and metallically. 'You heard a voice. I see.'

'Mustn't argue with Vawn's voices,' Ispex said.

'Voices from the Great Beyond,' Makenzi said. 'The voice from Illimitable Space! I hear it calling me! It's saying, "Makenzi! Why are you so beautiful?" '

Vawn hid her face in her hair and said, 'I heard it. Laugh as much as you like, I heard it and that's what it said. *We* built this place. Earth people, I mean. So you can all shut up.'

'All right, we'll shut up,' said Tsu, nastily. 'We'll get on to Any Other Business. Ispex, how are we getting on? Food and drink and stuff?'

Ispex said, 'Never mind about that. Shambles can synthesise protein from all this greenstuff. And extract water. We need *tools*, metals and any Earthstyle junk we can pick up. Tools, raw materials, that's what matters. We've got to *think* and *act*. If we don't soon find metals and Earthstyle artefacts, we'll be stuck here for *life* –'

'Or death,' Tsu said. 'A good place for dying, Moloch. All those things outside, just waiting to pick our bones . . . All those things we can't see, but they can see us. For all we know, we're being watched now! I mean, we've seen big creatures, but supposing there are some that are very small? Small enough to get in here?'

'If only we spoke to our parents,' Vawn began.

Makenzi broke in. 'I'm going out. Going hunting. Watching us, are they? Then let them watch out! Because I'm going looking for *them* –'

'You're supposed to hunt for *metals* and *artefacts*,' Ispex said.

'That, too. But I'm going hunting for pleasure,' Makenzi said. 'Just to show who's boss. Anyone want to come with me?'

Ispex pursed his lips. Vawn said, 'The only animal I'll hunt for is Fang.' She sniffed and swept out.

Tsu licked her lips and said, 'Come on, then, Mak. A-hunting we will go.'

HUNTERS

The light in the jungle never faded. There was no day, no night, only a darkening. No one could account for this. No one really tried. There were so many other things to think about.

As Tsu and Makenzi set out on their first hunting foray, the light was at its dimmest. The greens were dusky, sometimes luminous. Only the beads of water dripping from the plants were bright – startlingly bright.

It was silent, apart from the falling droplets. Their own footsteps sounded loud and clumsy to the hunters. Soon they learned to walk more silently. Later, they moved with hardly any sound at all; moved without talking, hardly breathing, until Tsu hissed, 'Eyes! Over there!'

They stood stock still, back to back, moving their heads very slowly and staring. Makenzi felt his heart pumping. He liked the feeling and knew that Tsu shared it. Buried inside him, there was the knowledge that he had done this before – not he himself, but his father and grandfather, his ancestors. They had stalked their prey in other jungles. But every jungle was the same. There was you, the hunter: and there was it, the prey. *You* killed *it*.

Tsu's elbow nudged his back, very gently. 'Turn,' she said. He turned and saw red eyes. They did not move. His heart beat even faster. His right hand very slowly raised a weapon. 'Stun,' he whispered to Tsu. 'You be ready with your Burner.'

The eyes blinked and moved. Instantly, Makenzi aimed and fired. The Stun cracked like a whip. It did not have a powerful charge in its cartridge. It did not need one. The bullet itself was what mattered. When it hit, it paralysed.

'*P-chak*!' said the Stun – and the red eyes suddenly became a wild beast, charging at them, tearing the mash of rotten vegetation under its great claws. The fur on its spine bristled and ruffed. Its mouth was red and wet and its teeth curved and white.

'*Burner*!' yelled Makenzi. But before Tsu could use it, the beast was almost on Makenzi, charging. He gripped his spear. Its point did not waver. The beast flung itself on to the point and the point thrust into its throat. As it thrust, he said, 'Ha!' and rammed the spear deeper.

The beast fell over as both the Stun and the spear took effect; and suddenly it was dead.

Makenzi clamped his big hands round Tsu's waist and lifted her into the air. 'Great! Glorious!' he shouted, trying to dance her above his head. His face was all teeth and eyes and ecstasy. 'Dead!' he shouted. 'Killed it dead!'

'Dead!' she shouted back. Her lips were twisted in a smiling snarl.

He let her down and they danced round each other. Then they inspected the kill. It was a sort of jackal, but with clumsy hooves that spread out to become rough claws. The canine teeth in its gaping, bloody mouth were so big that they had long ago bruised and cut the flesh round the opposing jaw. There were the beginnings of horny plates mixed with the coarse hair of its spine.

They stared at it for many minutes, admiring it. It was theirs now. They had made it theirs by killing it. Makenzi felt flooded with warmth for Tsu. They were sister and brother – no, twins. 'We'll do it again,' Tsu told him, looking into his face with eyes that were all blackness. 'Again!' he agreed, nodding and smiling. 'And again and again!'

Now the dead creature no longer interested them. They checked their weapons and without a word, set off once more into the depths of the jungle. They killed again and again, just as Makenzi said. At first they used Stun and Burner: later, only spears. Finally they used the spears to pin their prey, then went to work with hatchet and cleaver and knives, gasping and grunting as the bright steel rose and fell.

After many hours, they grew tired. They spitted their trophies on a spear, hoisted the spear on their shoulders and started for home. The spears bent with the weight of dead creatures. As they walked, they looked for the jellyfish things that waited high above them. When they saw one, they used their Burners and watched the jelly melt and fall, slobbering.

In *Starstormer*, Vawn and Ispex picked up the laughter of the hunters long before they arrived.

* * *

Vawn could not even speak when Makenzi and Tsu came in. She gasped, choked and fled.

Ispex said, 'Have you seen yourselves? You're dis-gust-ing! Obscene! Blood all over you!'

'Bedabbled with gore,' Tsu said happily. 'Bloodbath.'

'Wait till you see our trophies,' Makenzi boasted.

'I've got the exterior TVs working again,' Ispex said, stiffly. 'I have *also* set up a better aerial for the radio. I have *also* got the Navplan halfway working, all we need is tools and metals –'.

'She just lunged forward,' Makenzi said. 'Lunged forward with her spear, and *squirk!* –'

'Metals,' Ispex said. 'We need bits and pieces, nuts and bolts, anything you can find. We've got to have them.'

'We didn't even use spears at the end,' Tsu said. 'Not for the killing –'

'Listen,' Ispex said. 'We *don't* need dead animals. We *do* need Earthstyle leftovers. Next time you go hunting, hunt for them and never mind playing games.'

'P-pardon, you omitted to mention capacitors,' Shambles said. 'We must have capacitors, otherwise the Navplan –'

But Tsu and Makenzi were not listening.

Eventually they went away to clean themselves, giggling and shoving each other. Ispex stared after them, sighed, shrugged and told Shambles, 'We'll have another go at the radio. You sweep the frequencies, I'll fiddle with the aerial.'

He worked, bit his lip and worried.

VAWN'S JOURNEY

Alone, lying on her bed, Vawn forced herself not to think of Tsu and Makenzi. She made herself concentrate on fieldmice and the voices she had heard, the voices of Moloch. She was good at the trick of cutting herself off. Quite soon, her mind became clouded with jungle green and small bright eyes. She held long imaginary conversations with the little animals.

Above her head, a little box made a continuous humming noise. The box, battered and second-hand like everything else on *Starstormer*, contained a loudspeaker. It sent out voices not far from her: Ispex was saying, 'Try now, Tsu,' and Tsu replied, 'Still no go'. The box repeated these words, but so faintly that Vawn hardly heard them. The voices from outside – the Moloch voices – and the human voices were mixed up. Vawn concentrated on what she wanted to hear, the words in her mind.

'We will be your friends,' the mice squeaked, tinnily.

'Friendsss,' said the kind voices, soothingly.

'OK, Shambles. Try another sweep,' said Ispex, only half heard by Vawn.

'We'll have such fun together,' said the mice. 'We'll show you our homes, all warm and padded and private.'

'Hold it!' said Tsu, inaudibly. 'We're getting something!'

'You shall see for yourself,' promised the voices. 'Strange and wonderful thingsss –'

'Tsu! You're right! We're getting something! Lock on to it, Shambles!' said Ispex, so loudly that Vawn put her hands over her ears.

'A strange world, oursss,' said the voices in Vawn's head. Their music was like small waves sweeping a shingled beach.

'P-pardon,' said Shambles. 'But that signal, those voices, do not come from Epsilon Cool. They are from a source close to us. Very close.'

Vawn said to the mice, 'That's right. Come and sit on my lap, all of you. Clean your whiskers.' She was half asleep and her mouth smiled lazily.

The voices from Moloch said, 'Can you see it now? Can you? This is our world. Look, Vawn, look!'

Half dreaming, she looked and saw the voices' world as if from a spaceship, very low, very fast. In this ship, she passed over a small, circular jewel-like thing, a green and luminous ring. But it was soon gone.

Then the ship was rushing over another, bigger place with strangely lit red rocks and purple haze, still green lakes fringed with trees that dipped their branches in the water to feed . . .

And creatures, some of them in herds, by the lakes, some of them running across the plains, such strange animals . . .

And look! – she glimpsed a ring of animals clustered round some big creature lying on its side, they were doing things to it, horrible things, but then it was gone . . .

And then the spaceship went black, the light was gone, she was in a tunnel, a cave, a dark place, hurtling through it . . .

'*Usss*!' sang the voices. The spaceship stopped and she had arrived. This was the centre of their world, whoever they were. This was where the voices came from.

It was beautiful. In the great rocky cavern, bands and ribbons and sheets of coloured light were laid and overlaid like some great field of moving tapestry. Shimmering, living, singing pastures of light and colour.

'What is it?' Vawn whispered.

'*Usss*.' answered the voices.

'What are you?' she said.

'Good,' sang the voices. 'Good and wise.'

But Vawn remembered what she had seen – the ring of beasts encircling a victim. 'But –' she began.

The voices sang their answer before she could finish the question. 'There are evil things too,' they said. 'Evil and wise.'

'I don't understand,' Vawn said. 'Where are my friends, and *Starstormer*, and Fang? Are they here where you are?'

'Not here,' answered the voices. 'Very close, but not here. Did you not see the ring? The green ring? That is where you –'

'Hell's bells! Shambles, you moron!' said Ispex's voice, very loud and real. 'You've gone and lost it! Just when we had a good signal! –'

'P-pardon, I did not intend –'

Their angry voices rattled the little speaker. Vawn was at once properly awake, back in *Starstormer*. Yet the musical voices were still in her mind, and the floating bands of luminous, coloured tapestry, the centre of the world of the good and wise.

VOICES FROM HOME

The Starstormers crouched round the radio, staring at it, willing it to obey them. From the speakers, they heard space crackle, howl, whine, hoot, flutter, whistle. But they did not hear Epsilon Cool. They did not hear the voices of their parents.

Tsu said, 'Look, this has been going on for hours . . . I mean, even Fang could do better than this!' The little cat was on her lap, blinking. Rhythmically, it flexed its paws and dug its claws into her thigh. She took no notice. All her attention was on the radio.

'WE GOT YOUR –' the speakers bellowed: then were silent.

'Again! Just there!' Vawn said. 'You almost had it!' In a whisper to Ispex, she said, 'That sounded like Meg, your mother!'

He waved her away and scowled through his glasses at the radio. 'Come on, come *on*!' he said.

Suddenly it was unmistakably Meg, her voice high and worried. 'Don't give up sending, whatever you do!' she was saying. 'There's always one of us here, waiting . . . waiting to hear from you, always waiting . . . Clyde, you take over, just keep talking –'

Now it was Ispex's father Clyde. When he spoke, the Starstormers seemed almost to see the face behind the voice – solid, solemn, sandy, sensible, like Ispex. 'I'll begin, as usual, by giving you your Navplan fix . . .'

Scarlet-faced, Ispex said, 'It's him, him, him!' He reached out as if he would grab the radio and hold it to him.

'Got that fix?' Makenzi said to Shambles.

'Yes. It corresponds with mine. We are, as I told you, on Moloch.'

Briefly, the messages flowed back and forth. Makenzi spoke to his parents, Jass and Verona; Vawn to hers – Sheila and Dexter. Even Fang mewed across space, and the Starstormers laughed and heard laughter.

But then space lowered the curtain again and mocked them with hoots and crackles, birdcalls and echoing nonsense; and the true and real world of Epsilon Cool was gone, together with the people on it.

There remained the riddle of the Starstormers' world – the real world of here and now.

Vawn thought about it. What had the voices said? There had been talking mice, singing pastures . . . No, nobody would want to know about those! They'd laugh at her.

And the feeling of being watched by something evil – not just strange and ferocious beasts, something much worse – they wouldn't listen to her if she spoke of that.

But the ring, the little green ring she had seen . . . She had to tell someone about it. She told Ispex. 'This place is just a little ring, like an earring!' she announced; and waited for him to jeer.

He did not. He just stared back at her, solemnly,

and said, 'Could be.' Then nodded twice and went on his way.

* * *

Next day, the Starstormers feasted on fresh meat brought by the hunters. Vawn and Ispex pulled disapproving faces. But when they smelled the beautiful cooking smells, they were conquered.

As they ate, they talked. 'The funny thing was,' Tsu said, 'that although Mak and I kept on walking and walking, all those hours, at the end we seemed to be where we were at the beginning. I kept recognising things. Small things, a clump of vegetation, a particular tree. Or perhaps I didn't, I just thought I did, I don't know.'

Ispex said, 'What? What?' and looked up sharply.

Vawn, relaxed and full of food, looked smug and said, 'It's a small world.'

'What's that supposed to mean?' Tsu demanded.

'Vawn's got a theory about this place,' Ispex said. 'Some notion that this isn't a world at all, it's just a thing, a ring-shaped thing –'

'A ring thing,' Tsu said, sarcastically. '*Very* interesting. Kindly pass the salt, Vawn.'

Vawn began to fluster and bluster. 'You all laugh at me,' she said. 'But I'm the only one who's actually heard! – actually been in touch with them! – actually *talked* with them! –'

'Talked with whom?' Tsu said. Aside, to

Makenzi, she said, 'Here we go again! Vawn and her voices!'

'But I did hear them! I did! –'

'Shut up, Tsu,' Ispex said. 'Tell them, Vawn. Tell them the lot. I didn't believe it, but it begins to make sense now that Tsu says she's been walking in circles – Tell them, Vawn.'

So Vawn told them.

VAWN'S STORY

When she started her story, Vawn did her usual trick of hiding her face behind her hair, not wanting to see Tsu's scornful, golden mask or Makenzi's politely bored face. 'Well,' she said, 'I heard a voice, sort of. It was when I left the ship, you remember, to be on my own. And you came looking for me. And I was talking to the fieldmice –'

'Talking to the fieldmice,' Tsu said. 'How cosy.' Ispex nudged her savagely to silence her.

'– I was talking to the mice, and then I thought I heard a sort of wind, like a voice, like music, and this voice spoke to me. And I was taken on a trip –'

'Drugs?' Tsu enquired sweetly. But Ispex nudged her so hard that she said 'Ouch!' and stayed quiet.

Vawn did not notice. She was interested in her own story now. Her face had come out from behind the cloud of hair. 'I wasn't in this place, I was somewhere else, somewhere quite different,' she said. 'It was a world, a real, proper one. I saw it, I passed over it. I don't know how. And I went into a sort of cave where the rulers were, in the cave, and they told me that the world we are in was nothing to do with Tyrannopolis and nothing to do with *their* world: they said this place where we are now, it's *ours*. Humans made it. And perhaps I saw it, I don't know. Like a ring –'

'Ring thing. Ding-a-ling,' Tsu said, acidly.

'I think Vawn's right,' said Ispex, stubbornly.

'You believe in fairy rings?' Tsu said.

'You lot never *think*,' Ispex replied. 'But I do. I think Vawn's voices make sense. I think this place we're in really could be *ours* – I mean, we made it, it's an Earthstyle place made by humans. Consider the evidence.' He ticked the points off one by one on his fingers. 'First, Earthstyle vegetation. Oh, I know it's all gone wrong, but it's still plants and trees and creepers and mosses. Second, the animals. They're all wrong too, but they're Earthstyle nevertheless. You see a bit of dog here, a bit of jellyfish there . . . hair and hoof and horn, all the Earthstyle things. And third –'

'But how did they *get* here?' Tsu said, impatiently.

'I was just coming to that. If Vawn's voices and my theories are right, this isn't the planet of the Evil Eye or anything stupid like that. It's a sat-ellite! A ring satellite! It was put into space by humans! It drifted around for years. It entered the gravitational field of a real world, a big planet, and got pulled towards it. At last it stuck to it, like a pimple, and there we are.'

Tsu hissed gently between her teeth. She said, 'Yes! That's it! It's got to be that! Don't you see, we've got used to the way everything curves when you look into the distance! . . . Sort of curves away, like a tunnel. I *did* recognise the same things when Makenzi and I had done that long walk! I really *did*, because we'd walked right round the ring satellite and come back to the point we started from!'

'Wait!' Makenzi said. 'What about the creatures? They're all crazy monsters, how did they become like that? And why?'

Ispex sternly held up his bone to silence him. 'I hadn't finished,' he said. 'There's more evidence. Tell them, Shambles.'

Shambles said, 'As you know, Ispex is anxious to find any useful raw materials that may assist us in repairing *Starstormer*. He wants metal objects. He directed me to probe, by all the numerous means at my disposal –'

Tsu said, 'All right, all right, did you *find* anything?'

'He got several metallic traces and echoes,' Ispex said. 'Some could be aluminium, others could be ferrites, steels. Exactly the things we need to repair *Starstormer*,' he added, severely.

Makenzi said, 'Well, all right, you don't have to nag. We'll go out and hunt for them.'

Shambles interrupted, 'Almost certainly we are situated within a metallic structure. The responses to my probings indicate a regular lattice-like pattern surrounding us.'

'Ring satellite,' Tsu said, soberly. 'Fantastic. Here we are in what looks like and feels like and smells like a jungle and all the time it's a little Earthstyle doughnut in space . . .'

'Put up in space by humans,' Ispex said. 'Made by humans. And planted with Earthstyle plants, stocked with Earthstyle animals. I think this place was a sort of *en-vir-on-mental experiment*.'

'A Noah's Ark in space,' Vawn said. 'The animals went in two by two and –'

'They all went barmy and mutated,' Makenzi said. He rubbed his forehead. 'I don't get it. Why?'

'Why don't you do some *real* hunting?' Ispex said. 'Why don't you do what I'm always asking you to do – go and get some solid evidence for us to analyse, instead of killing the animals?'

'Why don't you boil your head?' Makenzi began. But Tsu cut him short.

'Ispex is right,' she said. 'We'll do it.'

* * *

Makenzi and Tsu went hunting. This time they carried metal detectors, sonic searchers and all the equipment needed to help them find metals and technical leftovers.

Above and all around them, the jungle dripped and rustled. Eyes watched and feet suddenly scurried. Tsu fingered the handle of her meat axe. She looked at Makenzi and raised an eyebrow. He said, 'No, we mustn't. Metals, not mutants.'

She sighed and said, 'All right. Let's get the gear set up and tuned.'

They need hardly have bothered with the fine tuning. The signals were so strong that the equipment instantly produced a symphony orchestra of squeaks, howls, blips and read-outs.

'Metals everywhere!' Makenzi said. 'All over the place! How are we going to sort this lot out?'

'Look for patterns?' Tsu suggested. She let her metal detector lead her, stamping her feet as she walked, flattening the damp grasses and mosses. She and Makenzi looked at the pattern her feet left. There were big diamond shapes, very regular, trodden into the ground. 'That proves it,' she said. 'This must be a ring satellite. Lots of standard diamond shapes all joined together –'

'And man-made, Earthstyle,' Makenzi said. He showed her the pale green readout of his analyst machine. It said, in plain written words, 'Iron . . . Chromium . . . Manganese . . .' and half a dozen more words, all familiar.

Tsu said, 'Look, Mak. My machine's trying to say something.' The machine in her hand, a directional detector, was making whining noises as she swung it ahead of her. The whining rose and fell, then became an unchanging, excited '*Wheeee!*' 'Sounds like a canary in ecstasy,' she said. 'Shall we follow it up?'

She held the detector in front of her like a magic wand and the two of them followed it, letting themselves be guided.

* * *

When Makenzi and Tsu left on their exploration, Ispex watched them go through an RV window and pouted. 'I ought to be out there,' he said to Vawn. 'I never get out of this ship.'

Vawn was combing Fang and did not bother to look up. 'You always say that,' she said, 'but you never actually go. You're scared.'

'I'm not scared! It's just that *someone* reliable must always remain on guard in the ship! –'

‘Scared,’ she said, calmly.

‘I don’t see *you* in any big hurry to go out there!’ he said, hotly, but she merely said, ‘Does he have lovely little paddy paws, then, and does he love his muvver best?’ Then, ‘I did go out, on my own. Don’t you remember? And I told you about this place. I discovered its secret. *You* didn’t. You all thought I was stupid. You always do, you’re all so dim. But I was proved right about all kinds of things –’

‘Oh, yes, of course! I suppose you can prove these *voices* you say you heard? – and the layers of coloured stuff or whatever it was in the cave, if there *was* a cave?’

She looked up from the cat and said, ‘I once heard the voices through the loudspeaker over my bed. Or I thought I did. I don’t really know. I was concentrating hard, I often do, trying to get in touch. At night. And I thought I heard the voices through the loudspeaker.’

‘Through the speaker?’ Ispex said. ‘Not just in your head?’

‘Yes. I was concentrating very hard.’

‘Only once?’

‘Once, twice – I don’t know. I go sort of dozy.’

‘You’re always sort of dozy. No, I don’t mean that, I apologise. Does it have to be in the night?’

‘Well, there isn’t any night, is there? I mean, when we sleep. I could do it now, I suppose.’

‘Do it, then!’ Ispex said, urgently. ‘Go on, Vawn, have a go! Try and get in touch!’

‘You’ll get all sarcastic if it doesn’t work, I know you! –’

'Try it. Lie down over there, go on. Close your eyes and try.' Shambles was near him. He prodded the robot's sides and muttered, 'Search the frequencies, Shambles. Keep searching and hold on any signal coming from close by. OK?'

Vawn closed her eyes, put Fang on her chest and stroked him. Fang blinked, smirked and settled his front paws into little loops. Shambles, like Ispex, stayed completely still.

For a long time, nothing moved and nothing happened.

* * *

But then the voices came. There were several. They filled Vawn's head and whispered tinnily in the loudspeakers so that Ispex could half-hear them too.

'Yesss?' said the musical voices, encouragingly.

'It's me, Vawn.'

'Yesss?'

'I – I just wanted to talk to you. About things. I don't know –'

'Yesss?'

'Ask about their planet,' Ispex said, urgently. 'Ask about Moloch, and the Evil Eye, and all the weird animals!'

'But you already know,' said the choir of musical voices. They sounded amused. 'You gave our planet the name Moloch, because you fear evil. We have another name for it, a name that means good.'

'Which name is right?' said Vawn. Her voice

was high and vague and sleepy.

'Both,' the voices replied.

In the distance, Ispex heard the noises made by Makenzi and Tsu, returning from their hunting expedition. Vawn heard too and twitched. Ispex cursed silently.

'Ask about *this* place, the place we're on?' Ispex said, frowning furiously and urgently. 'Find out, Vawn!'

The voices seemed to have heard him. 'Your world is your world, made by you. You humans. You put it into space, bit by bit – then assembled it.'

'And then what happened?' Vawn said.

'You're little world was drawn to our greater world. At last the two came together. But you know all thisss –'

'The creatures, the monsters!' Ipex hissed. 'Ask about them!'

Again, the voices seemed to have heard him. 'Yoursss!' it said. 'In the beginning, they were yours. Your beasts and insects and flying creatures. And your plants and herbs, trees and grasses. All of them yours – at first . . .'

'Noah's Ark,' Ispex muttered. 'Thought so.'

'You have living things too,' Vawn said, sleepily, to the voices. 'You showed them to me. When I flew. You did, didn't you? Or was it a dream?'

'Not a dream,' sang the voices. 'Not a vision. You saw what there was to see. Our good and our bad.'

'You are good,' Vawn said, with sleepy certainty.

'Good, good,' said the voices. 'But weak –' The music fell into sadness. 'We have not your powers.' the voices said. 'We are minds, merely minds – We rule, yet are powerless to enforce.'

Now Makenzi and Tsu were making rattling metallic noises: their hunting gear. To blanket the noise, Ispex said loudly 'Doesn't make sense! I mean, if you *rule*, you must have powers to enforce! I mean, *think* –'

Vawn said, 'No, you don't understand, Ispex. They're like a farmer, yes that's it, a farmer . . .' She seemed to have fixed her mind on the voices; they were telling her what to say. 'Like a farmer who becomes ill. He knows what's happening on his farm – to the beasts and the crops – but he can't *do* anything himself. So he sees everything going wrong –'

'He's got farm-workers,' said Ispex. 'Why can't he tell them what to do? Why can't he –'

The voices broke through his words. '*Now* we have farm-workers,' they said, 'now we have *you*!'

'*Us*?' Ispex exclaimed, completely puzzled.

But Vawn, still listening to the voices, said, 'Yes – yes – oh, I see! That's what you want!' Then she said, 'Oh, but we're not! You can't think that! We're not like that at all!'

She was so amazed by what the voices said that she sat up, wide awake. And the voices were gone.

'What did they say?' Ispex demanded.

'They were *rude*!' Vawn said, deeply shocked. 'Disgusting! Fancy saying that about us! Calling us *murderers*!' Fang leapt on her bed. She clutched him to her and said, 'Was oo mummy a murderer, den?'

Ispex snorted with disgust. 'Cut the baby talk and tell me what they *said*!' he shouted.

She said, 'Is that Mak and Tsu? What a racket they make. The voices . . . they said – it's a bit complicated – they said there's always been a sort of balance on Moloch – a balance between good and bad creatures. And the voices are just the sort of controlling brain in the middle, trying to keep the balance right. And it worked for millions of years.

'But then we put this Noah's-Ark ring satellite into space. It got stuck to Moloch because of Moloch's gravitational pull. Some of Moloch animals got in among the Earthstyle animals and there was crossbreeding –'

'Crossbreeding!' Ispex said. 'That explains the mutants!'

'Yes, that's right. Our Earthstyle animals went wonky. Only it was worse than that. The evil strains on Moloch at last found a way to show their power. I mean, the voices could control the evil forces on Moloch itself – but this place was a sort of leak, and the evil things leaked into it and took control, and the voices couldn't do anything about it. And now the evil things are winning.' She bit her lip, thinking about what she had said; then added, 'There really is an Evil Eye after all, you see. No wonder the voices are worried. But that doesn't excuse them calling us murderers, does it?'

'Tell me why they call us *murderers*,' said Ispex,

being very patient.

'Well, I mean, think how Tsu and Makenzi have been acting! Those hunting trips. All those animals they killed. *Disgusting*. I mean Tsu and Makenzi turned into murderers, didn't they?'

'So?'

'It's obvious. They're just what the voices want. Some murderers.'

'They *want* murderers?'

'Yes, of course. The voices said, "You humans are the most dangerous and murderous species known throughout the Galaxy!" '

Ispex said, 'Cheek!' Then he bit his lip, thought hard, and said, 'I suppose we are, at that. So what?'

'They want us to kill off as many evil creatures as possible. What they call "restoring the balance". The more baddies we kill, the better. Isn't that disgusting?'

'Not in the least. So we do their murdering for them . . . What do they do for us?'

'When we kill enough baddies, they help us find things we need. Even power to refuel *Starstormer*, anything.'

Ispex continued to bite his lip. He said, 'All right then. All right!' and strode from the bedroom, nodding his head in a satisfied way.

'Makenzi! Tsu!' he shouted. 'Where are you? I've something to tell you.'

'We're here. What is it?'

Ispex found them sharpening their hunting weapons. There was dried blood on their legs.

'We did your sort of hunting most of the time,'

Tsu said, shiftily.

'No need to look guilty,' Ispex told her. 'According to Vawn, bloodthirsty hunting is suddenly OK. In fact, you've *got* to hunt. OK?'

'OK,' Tsu said; and licked her lips.

MURDERERS

'*Huh*!' Makenzi said. It was not a word, only a tiny explosive sound. But by now, Tsu could understand his sounds perfectly, just as he understood hers. The 'Huh!' meant many things: something over there, where my head and eyes are pointing; something alive: something to be killed.

She gave a snake-like hiss noise in reply. 'I see it,' the noise said. 'My weapons are ready, my body is ready. Everything is ready for the killing.'

In the green darkness of the jungle, only their eyes shone. The rest of them was daubed and dulled with a dozen colours. They rubbed themselves with certain leaves that left green or purple stains; boiled plants and carcases to make dyes; stole ointments from the first-aid cabinet to smear themselves with – the oil made dried blood stick like greasepaint. And so Makenzi's black body became a tapestry of many lighter shades and Tsu's golden skin was patched with the colours of the jungle shadows.

Their warpaint was their only clothing except for the belts and crossbands, made from the skins of their prey, that held their supplies and weapons. They were hardened hunters now. They knew where to find water, which parts of their prey could be cooked and eaten. They carried only one weapon from the ship – a Burner. They used it to light cooking fires.

Their chosen weapons were bows and arrows made from aerials, spears made from knives honed razor-sharp, bound to shafts cut in the jungle, meat-axes from the kitchen – anything that stabbed or slashed.

'Tsss!' Tsu hissed, jabbing at her own chest with a finger. Makenzi rolled furious eyes at her – it was his turn to kill – but she repeated the sound and moved forward. She wanted to make the kill, it was to be hers.

He clawed at her with his big hand, trying to stop her but she was too quick. He saw her arm curve and swing and her spear, trembling as it flew, slither into the greenery – then her spider-like leaping as she followed the spear – then splintering, thumping blows of her meat chopper and the little gasping hisses of her breath as she finished – and last of all, the single word, like a deep purr.

'Ah . . . !' she said, deep in her throat. 'Ahhh.'

She came out of the undergrowth dragging her prey.

Makenzi still stared at her, furious. She said, almost apologetically, 'It's only a dango. Look.' He was not appeased. Even if it was only a dango, it was his turn, his dango.

'You'd no right –' he said, eyeing the limp body. 'It was *mine*.'

She answered by bringing down her chopper and neatly cutting off both hind legs – the only parts of a dango worth eating. 'Yours,' she said, holding them out.

He sneered. 'Who needs a dango,' he said and

knocked the legs out of her hands. 'Come on. We'll go for something interesting. Only remember, it's me first. The next one's mine.'

She smiled slantingly at him, found the severed legs and said, 'Pity to waste them. Bait.' She was right, of course. Blobs would fall from the trees to eat the bait. They might have fun spearing the blobs, watching them squirt and ooze.

Or better still, something big might take the bait. Something that would put up a fight – a tusker or a blinder or a crazy hog. They knew many of the creatures of the jungle now, and had given them names. But there were still some yet to be named. Killed first, named afterwards.

'OK,' Makenzi said. 'This way.' He deliberately left her to carry, alone, the long pole, padded with rolled sleeping bags, on which they spitted their prey. Usually they shared the burden, one at each end. Already the pole was heavy with bodies.

He strode ahead, animal tails bobbing and bouncing from his thong belt. She, as usual, continually darted her eyes from side to side as she walked.

Then Makenzi uttered his 'Huh!' and slithered silently to his knees, his head pointing at something she could not see. Immediately, she dropped too, silently placing the long spear on the ground. Slowly, she crawled to join Makenzi. She gave a hiss, meaning, 'What is it? Where is it?' He gave the slightest nod of his head towards a dark place. She saw what he saw: two staring eyes, set very wide apart.

'Big,' she murmured.

'My turn,' he replied, without turning his head.

And suddenly he was on his feet, his legs spread wide and the muscles of his body jumping under the painted skin – and his spear, quivering along its length, plunged into the darkness where the eyes glared –

The spear hit something and the thing bellowed: a single, coarse-throated, deep roar of rage. Then it was flying at them as if it had exploded from the ground, leathery jaws gaping, yellow teeth bared, fur bristling on the humped ridge of its neck where the spear stuck. The spear, two metres long, looked a toy now: a little stick that waggled in its bloody seating of fur and flesh.

The animal hit Makenzi and flattened him. Tsu saw the pale soles of Makenzi's dark feet, and the painted legs flailing, and the gaping pink hole of his mouth lined with white teeth. She had time to see all this, every detail of it, and hear his yell. Yet in the same instant she was off the ground, diving through the air, her left hand outstretched to grab the furry hide and her right raised with the razor-sharp meat-axe glinting.

She landed sprawled over the beast's back and the axe came down on the neck. It cut almost through the top of the spinal column with the first blow. The creature jerked its head back and reared. Makenzi was freed. As he rose, his knife thrust home between front leg and rib cage. He grunted and pushed the knife deeper. 'Die!' he snarled.

The creature did not die. It raised itself on its hind legs. Standing, it was taller than Makenzi. Its body was that of a huge wild dog – a hyena, a scavenging dog, a tufted, mangy hound. But its head was wide and heavy and huge, not like a dog's, the jaws were too enormous, the snarling, wrinkled muzzle too leathery and ape-like, the yellow teeth too blunt.

It stood, throwing Tsu off its back, and lashed out with a front paw. The blow sent Mak reeling and stumbling. 'Run!' he yelled to Tsu. 'Run!'

She did not run. She crouched, small and neat and tense. Strands of straight black hair striped her face. She stared at the beast, measuring angles and distances. The sums took her all of a second.

She shouted 'Hah!' – and sprang.

As the great animal turned to her she hit it in the throat with a hand clenching a knife. The beast yelled and clawed at nothing: Tsu was already gone. The beast roared again, its voice cracking. Makenzi saw a scarlet line growing at its throat. He flung his axe. It spun, flew and smacked into the beast's rib cage.

The beast, still standing, roared and staggered. Tsu spun her body in mid-air and kicked out backwards at its throat. The beast fell sideways and lay on the ground, panting.

Makenzi went to it and pulled the spear out of its neck. 'You,' he said, and offered the spear to Tsu. 'Yours.' His voice was thick and his eyes unsteady.

She said, 'No. It's your turn. Finish.'

He said, 'Right –' and thrust the spear through the beast's ribs. He drove the spear home with all his strength and whooped as it reached target: the heart.

* * *

Two hours later, when they had finished cooking and settled down to eat the choicest cuts of the beast, Tsu said, 'It's another mutation. They're all mutations.'

'You're right,' Makenzi said. 'Everything we've seen – everything but the Blobs – is Earthstyle. Earthstyle animals gone wrong.' He tore charred meat from a bone with his strong teeth. 'Good,' he said. 'Like roast lamb or something. Try it.'

She took the joint from him and bit into it. 'Oh yes,' she said. 'Good. If only we'd cut out the kidneys, I love kidneys. Do you want your bone back?'

'You finish it. You earned it.'

'We *both* earned it.'

They were happy with each other and everything else. Their fire had reached its ember stage. There were only small flames decorating the red glowing core, so hot that they sweated as they chewed and the blood on Tsu's heel was caked and crumbling. She contentedly eased off the dried blood with the toes of her other foot.

'Mutations,' said Makenzi. 'I wonder why?'

'You know why. Someone stocked this place with Earthstyle animals. A mutant strain got in somehow, and they started going wrong.'

'Or right. Perhaps the way they are suits this place. They could have changed for the better.'

'No, I don't think so. This creature we're eating . . .' She pointed at the tufted carcase with her bone. 'I mean, look at it! It doesn't look as if it suits itself, if you know what I mean. Earthstyle animals – penguins, mice, cats, horses – they all look as if they *had* to be that shape. While the creatures we kill, they're all somehow wrong and ugly. Wow, I've eaten all the meat off this bone and I'm still hungry.'

'Perhaps you're mutating,' Makenzi said, stretching. 'Perhaps you're becoming a pig.'

'Greedy pig,' she agreed. She lay back against her sleeping-bag roll. 'Biggest animal we've seen yet. Nice kill. Yet I keep getting the feeling there's something even bigger in the jungle. Watching. Waiting. A monster . . .'

Makenzi, not listening, said, 'You were terrific, Tsu. The way you back-kicked it –'

'I enjoyed that bit,' Tsu said, blinking sleepily. 'Kick! Whoompf!'

'No, seriously, Tsu. You were great.'

She would not listen. 'I want to sleep now,' she said. 'Pity about the kidneys.' They slept.

* * *

When Makenzi woke he found a way to show Tsu how he felt. He collected the right leaves and stalks, took blood and fat from the dead beast and mixed up some high quality warpaints.

When Tsu awoke, he said, 'Right. Stand up and don't move.' Then he did a really good paint job on her back – her legs and everything – while she attended to her front.

'Terrific,' she said when they both finished. And Makenzi was satisfied.

* * *

'Liver,' Vawn said, in a housewifely tone of voice, a few days later. 'Where's the liver? I hope you didn't forget. Fang must have his liver.'

She held out her hand to the painted savages, just returned from yet another hunt. Tsu slapped a dango's liver into the hand. 'There you are. Still warm.'

'How disgusting,' Vawn said, fastidiously. 'And the kidneys. What about them?'

'Can't have them,' Makenzi said. 'We're saving them for breakfast.'

'But Fang loves kidneys, doesn't oo, den?' Fang rubbed at Vawn's ankles and stretched upwards, grabbing with his claws at the liver in Vawn's hand. He said, 'Mrrr-aoww!' in a voice of strangled longing.

Ispex came in and said, 'Oh, you two are back. You look horrible. *A-bom-in-able.* Did you get any kidneys? We could have them for breakfast –'

Tsu said, 'Say please. Go on, Ispex. Say please, or we won't give you any.'

Ispex muttered something that was not 'please' and Tsu laughed at him while she absent-mindedly picked at a smear of caked blood on her painted thigh. Makenzi waggled kidneys in Ispex's face and said, 'Look, Ispex! Yum-yum! You like kidneys, don't you? And steaks? It's just the hunting you object to. So vulgar!'

Ispex said, 'I've been hunting. *Really* hunting. Come and see.'

He led the way to the little clearing that had become *Starstormer*'s backyard. The yard was piled high with metallic junk. 'Relays,' Ispex said, pointing a plump, sandy finger. 'Navplan modules. Capacitors. Booster cores –'

Shambles interrupted. 'P-pardon, but I think I have the Navplan functioning correctly,' he said. 'I have just completed a run-through with most sat-sat-satisfactory results –'

Tsu, no longer teasing, said, 'Where have you got to, Ispex?'

'Almost there,' he said, with grave satisfaction. 'We could fly *Starstormer* as she is now. And in another two or three days, she'd be better than ever she was. The TV system will be better – longer range, higher resolution. And she'll be more stable in flight because of this stuff.' He kicked a little shining box, whiskered with a hundred hair-fine wires. 'Navplan module. The stuff we had originally was junk –'

'But this is junk,' Makenzi said, looking suspiciously at the little box.

'Yes, but *better* junk,' Ispex said. 'Up-to-date.'

Makenzi stared at the business-like piles of equipment and said, 'Terrific, Ispex. Don't you think so, Tsu?'

'Terrific. You're a genius, Ispex.'

'That's because I *think*,' Ispex said, severely. 'Mind you save me some kidneys.'

ON THE SETTLEMENT

Above Epsilon Cool, the great dark spaceship from Tyrannopolis rested on its shimmering bolster of violet fire. The thunder of its power shook human brains and its vast mass darkened the sky.

Occasionally, little pin-pricks of light, pretty and innocent, decorated the sombre mass. The twinkling lights were gunfire. The humans flinched and waited for the familiar, hated, zipping sound as the small missiles tore into the bubble domes of the settlement.

'Why don't we fire back?' Verona muttered. 'Why don't we just blast their rotten ship –'

Her husband, Jass, said, 'You know the reason why. Be calm.'

'Calm!' shouted Vawn's mother, Sheila. 'He says, "Be calm!" All those years of work – *our* work! – being torn to pieces, bit by bit, and he says, "Be calm"! '

Ispex's father, Clyde, said, 'I know how you feel. And how *I* feel. But think, just think –'

The Voice of Tyrannopolis bellowed through the speakers and completed Clyde's argument. 'Obey! Obey the Emperor! Instruct your children to return! The Emperor wants your children! Obey the Emperor!'

'*I* want our children,' Sheila said, and began to cry, helplessly. 'Why can't we –'

'We are using our lightest weapons,' thundered the Voice. 'The Emperor has not yet begun to punish you! We are firing only our smallest missiles, inflicting the least possible damage to you and your settlement! But if you do not obey – if you do not surrender the children – then the Emperor will insist on sterner measures –'

'Why don't we just *smash* that ship!' Sheila shouted. 'Obliterate it! Wipe it out!'

'Because it wouldn't make the least difference,' Dexter said, wearily. 'The ship is nearly all dust. What's the point of disturbing dust?'

'But the weapons! –'

'The Emperor has more weapons, more ships, more of everything,' Dexter said. 'You know that. And if we surrender our children, he will use them to help him make still more weapons, even more deadly fighter ships.'

'But the Emperor will destroy everything we've built! Even kill us! –'

'Us, perhaps,' Jass said. 'Although I doubt it. We represent what he needs: human technology, human abilities. But he'll never destroy the children. They represent his *hands* –'

'Obey the Emperor!' the Voice bellowed.

Meg, mother of Ispex, had said nothing. She merely sat, plump and defeated. She flinched when the missiles hit. Now she stood up and said, in a hard voice that did not seem to be hers, 'I'm taking a holiday. A vacation. Anyone coming?'

The others stared at her. Jass said, very gently, 'Wait a minute, Meg. I'm not quite clear –'

'A holiday. I'm taking the shuttle and going to

Moloch and the children. I can't stand this any more. I must see Ispex and the children.'

Verona said, 'Meg, you can't. The Emperor's ship is out there and he's got fighter craft as well. You'd never get through.'

'The children did,' Meg said. 'They got *here*. They fought their way through. Remember?'

'And they knocked out the Emperor's fighters,' Dexter said, almost in a whisper. 'If *they* could do it, in *Starstormer* –'

'But the settlement!' Jass said, waving a hand at the equipment surrounding him. 'It's only by constant attention to this gear that we can keep the settlement going at all!'

Meg said, 'I'm going. Who's coming with me?'

There was a long silence, broken when Meg said, 'You just told us, Jass, that the Emperor doesn't want us dead – that he doesn't want the settlement destroyed: we and it are too valuable. All right, then. I'm taking a holiday. Visiting the children. For the last time, who's coming?'

Jass spoke. 'The only person here who thinks straight,' he said, 'is Meg. Let's load the shuttle.'

'Load it with what?' Dexter said.

'Weapons,' Jass said. 'All the weapons we've got. Come on!'

ARRIVALS

'They're on their way!' Makenzi croaked. His throat was squeezed shut with panic and excitement. 'The Epsilon Cool shuttle!' He jabbed a finger at a tiny green dot on the Navplan screen. 'That's them!' he said.

The Starstormers listened to the radio. It wheezed and whistled and howled. Ispex said, 'Out of my way!' and thrust one of Shambles' tentacles into the set. 'Scan, Shambles. Get us the best signal.' Shambles flickered lights and grumbled to himself in concentration. The voices came through.

'. . . Get a message to them somehow,' said the speakers, in Clyde's voice. Then – 'Try another scan. Jass, come over here, it's all noise –'

'They're looking for us,' breathed Ispex. 'Give them a beam, Shambles. Something they can't miss.'

Shambles beamed. Clyde's voice said, 'Ah! Ah! We've got a beam, they're sending –'

And all at once, the voices were very clear, as if the crew of the shuttle were right there in *Starstormer*. Ispex's face glowed: 'I put a new tranny block in,' he said. 'It's made a difference. A *considerable* difference. It was quite a tricky business –'

'Listen!' Vawn hissed.

'They're beaming really strongly,' Verona's voice said. 'Let's try sending, we can't miss! –'

But then the Starstormers heard Dexter's voice shout, deafeningly, 'Attack! Attack! Stations, everyone!'

There was a shattering roar so loud that the speakers rattled, and the howl of something moving very fast, and the bark of the shuttle's weapons, and voices shouting. The Starstormers heard Jass shout, 'It's their destroyers, I saw them on RV!' and the shuttle's weapons were louder. The Starstormers could even hear the sound of feet running and the little clicks of controls operated by impatient fingers. In the background, the attacking ships roared like lions – roared with notes that started high and sank low as the attackers hurtled past. One of the roars became a scream; then there was the thunder of a distant explosion; and Dexter was heard laughing wildly. 'Got him! Got him! he yelled.

Then Jass's triumphant voice: 'Ball of fire! You should see it! Here in the RV –'

And the Starstormers cheered too, knowing that the invisible battle was being won – that the Octopus Emperor's few human slaves could have made only a few destroyer craft – that they themselves might never be slaves if only their parents could win through – and best of all, that the shuttle was on its way, really on its way, closer every glorious second.

So they cheered every sound the speakers made. The hugged each other. Makenzi stood on his head. And so it went on until the mad nonsense of electronic noises in space invaded and swamped the radio.

*   *   *

Later – 'They've landed!' Makenzi said, hoarsely. 'They're here!'

'Where? Why can't I *see* them? Where are they?' Vawn cried.

Shambles said, 'P-pardon, they have landed 150 degrees from us. 150 degrees round the ring, clockwise.'

'Why didn't they land next to us, close to us? Why, why?'

Ispex guessed why. The Epsilon Cool shuttle must have been hit. Hit and damaged. Otherwise its crew would have brought it down next to *Starstormer* and made immediate radio contact.

He kept these thoughts to himself and said, 'Makenzi. Let's get out to them. At once. Who goes?'

Makenzi looked up, puzzled for a moment: but he very quickly read Ispex's face and guessed his thoughts. He said, 'Me and Tsu, no-one else.'

'But wait a minute!' Ispex protested. 'What about me? I want to go!'

'I want to go too!' Vawn burst out. 'I must! You can't stop me!'

'Just Tsu and me,' Makenzi said. 'Sorry, Vawn. Sorry, Ispex. Ready, Tsu?'

Vawn wept and pleaded. Ispex held her back. '*Think*, Vawn!' he said. 'You'd slow them down! *I'd* slow them down! Mak and Tsu know the jungle best!' Then – 'Hey, you two! – clockwise, remember!'

Tsu and Makenzi left in a hurry, their crude weapons in their hands, their arms and legs glinting greenly as they ran, fast but without haste, into the jungle.

'Radio, Vawn,' Ispex said. 'Keep searching for signals from the shuttle.' It was something to keep her busy. He squatted beside Shambles and stared at the read-outs on the robot's side. 'Track them, Shambles,' he muttered.

'Cer-certainly. Track whom?'

'Tsu and Makenzi, idiot. Follow each step they take.' Ispex was thinking of the mutant creatures, great and small, that infested the ring satellite. He thought of jelly-like blobs, waiting to drop; of red eyes and sharp yellow teeth hidden in undergrowth; of the Evil Eye that seemed to overlook everything and everyone.

'Follow each step they take,' he repeated.

IN THE SHUTTLE

'Well,' Jass said, trying to keep his voice steady, 'We made a landing.'

'Of sorts,' Clyde said. There was a gaping gash in his scalp, made when his helmet shattered. Blood from the gash poured over the left side of his face. 'Can't see properly,' he complained.

Meg said, 'Here. Let me.' She dusted yellow powder over the wound and pressed a medipad against it. The blood stopped.

Sheila said, 'This *is* the right place? It *is* the ring satellite? It had better be –' She looked dully around her. The one and only missile from the Tyrannopolis destroyers that had really hit, had caused havoc. The control cabin got the worst of it. It looked as much a jungle as the tangled greenery outside. Sheila saw twisted metal, smouldering wiring, smashed plastics.

She said, 'We must get a fix on *Starstormer*.'

'You're joking,' Verona replied, nodding her head in the direction of the radio and Navplan. Both were wrecked. 'We'll have to walk. Just walk and keep walking. This place is a ring, a circle, we're bound to find *Starstormer* eventually. *Starstormer* and the children –'

Jass said, 'Right, we walk. Who *can't* walk? Anyone?' They tried out their legs. Some hobbled, others limped, but all could walk.

'Weapons,' Clyde said. 'Small arms.' He handed out Stuns and hand guns. 'Everyone ready? OK, helmets on.'

'Wait a minute,' Jass said. 'Which way do we go? Left or right? Clockwise or anticlockwise?'

'Toss for it,' Dexter said. He spun a Stun cartridge. It was a disc marked only on one side. 'Rough is clockwise, smooth anticlockwise,' he said.

The disc spun in the air and landed. Dexter peered at it.

'Rough,' he announced. 'Off we go, then. Clockwise.'

Half an hour passed almost in silence as Vawn sniffed back tears and scanned the radio frequencies, hoping to pick up her parents; Ispex peered at the screens, keeping track of Tsu and Makenzi. 'They're going fast,' he told Vawn. 'They must be half running, half walking. Really covering the ground!'

She refused to be cheered. 'I want to speak to them,' she said, 'speak to my parents. I must know they're safe!'

Shambles said, 'P-pardon . . . I think I have located them. It must be them, unless, of course –'

Ispex said, 'Let me look!' and peered at the read-outs. The numbers on Shambles' flanks made no sense to him. 'Screen them!' Ispex ordered. Shambles presented a TV display in the form of a segment of a circle, an arc of brightness. The arc had confused, glittering points on it. They moved clockwise. Ispex tried to count them. He reached twenty and scratched his nose, puzzled. 'But six of them form a sort of steady knot,' he muttered to himself. 'They must be Jass and Verona, Meg, Sheila, Dexter, Clyde –'

'It's got to be them!' Vawn squealed. Her face was alight. Then it clouded. 'But what are the other dots?' she said.

'Oh, anything, anything at all,' Ispex said.

'False traces, anything.' He was lying. He knew what the other moving dots were most likely to be: wild beasts, circling and stalking the humans, waiting to pounce and kill. He felt a coldness creep over him.

He thought, 'I must match the dots I don't know with dots I *do* know.' So he made Shambles select another part of the circle – the arc containing Tsu and Makenzi.

Ah, there they were! Two moving dots, Makenzi and Tsu, quite definitely; moving steadily, clockwise, along the arc . . .

The coldness became a sudden icy chill. The other dots – they were moving clockwise too! So the two parties were following each other round the circle, never coming closer!

'Shambles, tell them!' he shouted. 'Tell Tsu and Makenzi they're heading the wrong way!'

'B-but that is impossible,' Shambles said. 'They are not carrying communication gear of any kind! They just took their weapons and hurried away.'

Ispex's jaw dropped. 'You mean, we can't speak to them?'

'I regret, no.'

Ispex said, 'Vawn. Quick. Find spears, hatchets, Stuns, anything. Those other dots! We've got to go out into the jungle!'

Vawn said, 'What? Why?' Then she understood. The other dots could be killers. Without a word, weapons in each hand, she ran into the jungle, her long legs leaving Ispex panting as he tried to keep up with her.

'What the devil!' said Jass. The blob had fallen from nowhere. He felt a great weight smashing down on his helmeted head; and all at once he was blinded by a curtain, still descending, of translucent slime. He gave a great shout of terror and shock.

Dexter used his Stun. The jelly-like blob flinched and quivered, yet kept spreading. Now it crept down over Jass's shoulders. Sheila hacked at it with a dagger, leaving wet, gaping wounds. The blob shivered – but still spread.

Another blob fell from above. It aimed for Clyde but missed him. It tried to spread itself over his boots. Verona blasted it with a *pow* and it crinkled and shrivelled.

'Look out!' Dexter shouted as an impossible beast, glaring-eyed, shot out and up from the undergrowth, clawed forelegs spread wide, eyes blazing, yellow fangs gaping. Somehow Meg brought her *pow* to bear on the monstrous thing and drilled a burning hole through it. Yet still it crawled towards them, eyes glazing, jaws dripping. She shot it again and it stopped.

Jass wrenched off his helmet and the blob that enveloped it. His hands were covered with a jelly-like slime. He backed away from the horror, eyes rolling and mouth working. His Stun pumped again and again into the heaving jelly. He did not see a snake-like tentacle whip from the roots of a thick-leafed shrub. The tentacle wrapped round his ankle.

Sheila saw it. She hacked through the tentacle with her dagger, screaming with furious terror as her arm flailed.

Somehow they made their way to a clearer place, not overhung with trees from which blobs might drop, not fringed with plants that might attack them in ways they could not imagine.

'Form a ring,' Clyde ordered. 'Back to back. Weapons facing out.' They obeyed, pulling Jass into his place – helmetless, he could not hear Clyde's words. They stood, weapons facing outwards. The muzzles of the weapons were not steady.

There was silence, except for rustlings in the undergrowth and Sheila's strangled sobs . . .

Then the rustling became an unmistakable sound, the noise of feet pounding and limbs thrashing through plants . . .

'Get ready!' Clyde said, tightening his finger on the trigger . . .

And then they were there, bursting out of the jungle and into the clearing . . .

Ispex and Vawn.

* * *

Makenzi and Tsu stopped running, fought for breath and stared. They had reached the Epsilon Cool shuttle. It had a ragged hole torn in it, fringed with burn marks. Its nose was enmeshed with a twisted lattice of geodetic framing torn from the structure of the doughnut ring when the shuttle had plunged through it to crash-land.

Makenzi said, 'Oh Lord! . . . Oh, Lord!' He clambered up the shattered hull and thrust his head into the ragged hole.

'Are they there?' Tsu shouted.

'They're not here, thank heaven. They must have got out safely and left.'

Tsu said, 'Then where *are* they?' Without waiting for an answer, she bent low to the ground and began moving like an animal on all-fours with her face close to the earth. She soon found what she was seeking.

'Here, Mak! Lots of tracks! This is where they stood around, deciding what to do next. They talked for some time, and got themselves equipped, then they took off–here we are, you can see. They went that way.'

'And we went the same way,' Makenzi said, miserably. 'The *wrong* way. Both been going round the same circle. Now what do we do?'

Again Tsu did not wait for an answer. She simply started running, following the tracks. They were as clear to her as printed words in a book. Makenzi followed, unhurried yet fast.

'Ninety-nine, a hundred,' Tsu murmured, and walked.

'Twenty-nine, thirty,' Makenzi said, and they ran. They could keep this up endlessly.

Green, snake-like tentacles whipped out at them. 'Oh, go away,' Tsu said peevishly, slashing through them without breaking her stride.

A tufted, hideous boar-like creature snapped at Makenzi's heels with razor teeth. He jumped over it and kept running.

A blob fell from above, but their experienced eyes spotted it before it had fallen a metre: it fell harmlessly on the wet ground.

'Ninety-nine, a hundred . . .'

'Twenty-nine, thirty . . .'

They travelled at least four times as fast as the party from the Epsilon Cool shuttle.

THE GREAT MONSTER

In the jungle clearing, the grim-faced crew of the shuttle dropped their weapons, opened their arms and embraced Vawn and Ispex. Vawn flung herself into her parents' arms. Ispex simply stood, scarlet-faced, his lower lip stuck out and trembling, until he was clutched and hugged and kissed and pounded on the back. He could not speak for whole minutes.

* * *

Twenty metres away from the humans, hooded eyes watched and a tongue slithered wetly over razor teeth. Raw, pig-like ears were laid back. On an enormously powerful hunched neck, coarse fur rose and bristled. Massive ridged hooves sank into soft, spongy earth, stealthily digging for a firm purchase when the beast launched itself.

The flanks quivered: the muscles of the great haunches tightened under the scaled and tufted hide; heavy breath whistled hoarsely through the wrinkled nostrils beneath the single horn, curved like a scimitar, polished at the sharpened point.

This was the Lord of the Monsters, the personification of the Evil Eye.

Ready for the kill.

* * *

Makenzi, sweat spraying from him with each step, said, 'Over there! Ahead! Didn't you hear! Voices!'

Tsu panted, 'Them . . . must be them . . . faster!' She twisted her face into a grin. Makenzi managed to grin back.

'Safe!' he gasped. 'Talking ordinarily! Keep running! They're safe!'

* * *

The Lord of the Monsters glared its evil eyes till they rolled in their yellowed whites – and sprang.

It covered the twenty metres in two great bounds. The ridged hooves sent earth flying.

The monster roared. Leaves quivered and strange birds screeched and flew.

The monster hit the group of humans as a bowling ball hits skittles. The group exploded into single flying bodies when the great blunt head and bulging shoulders smashed into it.

Jass, flung ten metres from where he had stood, lay on his side, mouth open, staring eyes stunned by what they saw – the enormous and hideous body, the glaring, rolling, wicked eyes, the slavering mouth. And the horn: the curved horn. Green light glinted on the polished tip. Jass's eyes tried dazedly to follow the glint.

Man and beast both made the same motion – a shaking of lowered heads. Jass was trying to clear his clouded brain: the beast's brain was completely clear. It would attack. It would kill. It began moving in a tight circle, shaking its head and horn, snorting furiously through wet, leathery nostrils, rolling its reddened eyes.

Meg was the first to come fully to her senses. She started crawling towards a Stun. 'Weapons!' she muttered. 'Get to the weapons!'

Because she moved, the beast decided to attack her. It trotted heavily towards her, taking its time, knowing how helpless was its victim. The muscles of its humped shoulders tightened and swelled. The power of the muscles quivered through the ridged muscles along the spine and reached the hind legs. The trot became a rush and the rush a charge.

Meg saw the great bulk rushing at her, darkening the jungle light. 'I thought, it's like me,' she told the others, later – 'like me, too clumsy, too heavy for its own good' and so she made herself wait for endless seconds while the beast set a course it could not turn from. At the last instant, she fell sideways and let herself roll.

The beast careered past, swinging its horned head sideways. The tip of the horn caught her suit and ripped it from waist to shoulders without even grazing her skin.

Not daring to look back, Meg again crawled, gasping, in the direction of the Stun. Behind her, the beast slammed and thrashed in the tangled stuff surrounding the clearing, trampling its way free. It bellowed in its rage.

Verona beat Meg to the Stun. She showed her white teeth at the monster and tucked the weapon into firing position. The monster was free now, free and coming at her, shaking the ground as it increased its speed. Verona's trigger finger tightened until a knuckle showed ivory against the dark skin. Nothing happened. The weapon was dead. She triggered it again and again then flung it with all her strength at the beast's head. It bounced off like a toy. Verona ran.

The others were recovered now. Dexter had a Burner. He aimed, fired and hit. There was a stench of burning hair. The monster shook its head as it ran, feeling the pain of the burn: but feeling too the burning delight of the killings to come, the lust for flesh and blood. That was the feeling that mattered. The Burner was nothing.

Meg, sobbing, groped for the Stun that Veronica had flung from her. 'It must work,' she told herself, 'it's *got* to work.' She pulled the trigger and the weapon spat. She clutched it to her shoulder, took uncertain aim at the monster – and fired. Her shot hit home. The bullet lodged in the beast's hind leg and jetted its paralysing agent.

That should have been enough. The beast should have checked – staggered – dropped. The Lord of the Monsters did not. It craned its head to find the wound. Its flank quivered as the drug took hold. It came to a halt and looked at its human enemies with puzzled eyes. But then the evil in it flared again and the beast was itself, shaking its furious head so that thick saliva was flung in glittering ropes. It raised its hump, lowered its head – and charged again.

Its target was Dexter. He was on his feet, braced with legs spread. He fired his Stun twice. One bullet hit – he saw the coarse flesh pucker. But then the beast was almost on him. Dexter threw himself aside, losing the Stun. The monster forgot the man and inspected the Stun. Dimly, it understood that pain came out of the thing. It put a hoof on the weapon, bore down, and crushed it into the soft ground.

Clyde, Ispex's father, stuck out his lower lip and muttered, 'Useless! Leave it to me!' He held a Burner.

Jass saw the plump, determined figure edge forward. 'Get back!' he shouted. 'Don't!' He knew Clyde was the wrong man for the job: Clyde looked somehow like a little boy wearing big boxing gloves. He frowned and moved nearer the monster, twisting and dodging as he tried to react to the beast's movements. Now no one dared fire weapons for fear of hitting him. 'Get back!' screamed Jass. Clyde jutted his lower lip and moved in. Then he did what Jass most feared: he fired the Burner.

At that range he could not miss. Hair burned and flesh seared. The monster gave a screaming bellow – and with astonishing speed, swung round on its hind legs to face Clyde. The beast towered over the man. The great horn swung, viciously. Clyde moved back – fired the Burner again – stumbled – fell. His shots burned holes, uselessly, in the canopy of trees and creepers above. The monster gaped its jaws, made a sound in its throat – a deep, rumbling, satisfied, triumphant sound – and lowered its horn over Clyde's writhing body.

Jass, his face twisted with fear for Clyde, ran at the monster. As he ran, he emptied the magazine of his old automatic pistol, a souvenir of the twentieth century. He carried it only because he liked the machined, blued steel. It was a toy.

Now the toy became something more. Its seven shots lanced into the hide of the monster, distracting it: and the noises confused it. It forgot Clyde and turned to the noises. Its brain was slow, but quick enough: and its horn was quicker still. It stumbled forward, ponderously at first but faster and faster, with the horn against Jass's chest. Jass clutched the horn and ran backwards – fast, too fast, impossibly fast. The monster bore on, its hump rising –

There were short, sharp screams, animal yelps, as Tsu and Makenzi burst out of the jungle and into the clearing.

* * *

They kept yelling. They knew the effect of these inhuman hunting cries. They were animal sounds that no animal recognised: sounds that were mysterious threats.

The monster heard, hesitated and slowed.

Makenzi yelled one word – 'Zigzag!' – and ran across the monster's head. As he ran he flung a spear. The monster checked –

Tsu ran in front of it from the opposite direction, screaming short yelps. She too sent a spear hurtling. It plunged into the beast's neck. The monster swung its head from side to side. It could not make sense of these new creatures that behaved so strangely.

Makenzi ran from behind the monster. He

snatched his spear out of its hide as he ran, then plunged it in again. As he ran, he yelled and pranced. The Lord of the Monsters turned in its own tracks, trying to understand.

Tsu, on its blind side, ran in and slashed three times with her hatchet at the beast's slab-sided neck. The blows were incredibly light and fast yet blood flowed thickly.

Makenzi picked up a *pow* on the run – and still running, fired. The front legs of the monster buckled. The head dropped and wagged. The evil eyes seemed astonished at first; then dull and fired with a dying glimmer of rage.

Tsu and Makenzi ran and struck, zigzagged and attacked, until the monster dropped on its front legs, roared for the last time, fell slowly and massively on its side, and died.

The last light faded from the Evil Eye.

THE CAVERN OF RADIANCE

They walked, all of them, on Moloch. It was like a Sunday outing back on Earth.

Tsu said, 'Giddy-up!' and dug her heels into Jass's ribs. She was astride his shoulders. She flourished a leafy branch and occasionally walloped him with it.

Jass said, 'That's cruelty to animals!'

'*Dumb* animals,' she replied cheerfully and threatened him again with her branch.

'You're heavier than you look,' Jass complained. 'Suppose you carry me for a change?'

'Bet she could, at that,' Verona laughed. She was arm in arm with Makenzi and Sheila. Sheila needed support. Her thigh had been bruised and her arm broken when the Lord of the Monsters made its first charge. The osteo-medipak in the shuttle hadn't been damaged, so the break would be mended in a week or so. And in any case, who cared? She had her daughter. And Moloch was a beautiful and interesting planet. To be free – and walking without a helmet – and together again . . . What did a broken arm matter?

Dexter and Ispex were a long way ahead of the main party. They had gulped down their food and refused to take a rest with the others. Ispex had said, 'Those rock formations indicate a deliberate, artificially applied environmental change –'

Dexter said, 'Nonsense. They don't.'

'They do. Def-in-ite-ly.'

'They don't.'

Arguing furiously, they tapped rocks with their special hammers and expounded theories.

'How far to the caves? – them – the voices – you know what I mean,' Sheila asked Vawn.

'I don't know exactly,' Vawn answered, in a matter-of-fact tone. 'I can hear the voices in my head all the time . . . They just say, "Come on, that's right, we're waiting to welcome you".'

Sheila looked sideways at her daughter and thought, 'She looks so sure and serene; she can't be making it all up, the voices, and everything. Oh, I do hope she isn't. I do so want her to be right. And to see what she has seen – if she *has* seen it –'

Clyde said, 'Vawn, look over there: could that be the place?'

He pointed at a low mountain, gold and purple and green in the strange slanting light that flooded the surface of the planet, picking out every growth on its rocky surface. In the mountain there was a dark place, the mouth of a cave. 'Could that be it?' Clyde said.

'Yes, that's it,' Vawn said.

'You're sure?' Clyde said.

'Of course. I've just asked the voices. We go there. Doesn't look far, does it?' She quickened her pace.

Clyde raised an eyebrow at Sheila and murmured, 'I hope that daughter of yours isn't leading us on a wild-goose chase, Sheila.'

'Of course she isn't,' Sheila said, sounding more

confident than she felt.

The party skirted a large outcrop of what appeared to be granite and came on Ispex and Dexter. They were holding bits of rock under each others' noses and arguing more furiously than ever. 'Stop it, you two,' Verona said. 'We're nearly there. Vawn says so. Behave yourselves and prepare to meet *them* . . . the masters of Moloch, or whatever . . .' She winked at Jass. He swung Tsu off his shoulders and on to her own feet. He looked up at the cave.

'Use your own muscles now,' he told Tsu. 'That's quite a steep climb.'

They laboured up the long ascent to the mouth of the cave. They saw birds fly in and out, strange birds that glittered as they emerged from the darkness into the light. Everyone looked at them except Sheila. She stared at her daughter's face.

Vawn was smiling, a quiet, sure smile. 'Those birds,' she said, 'This is the only cave they like! Strange isn't it? Just this cave and no other.'

Sheila was about to ask, 'How do you know that?' but decided not to. She knew what answer Vawn would have given.

They entered the cavern.

* * *

'Welcome,' sang the voices in the velvety, glowing darkness. 'Welcome to our home. Come closer. Closer still . . . You are very near to usss –'

A radiance glowed behind a jagged wall of rock.

The humans' faces were lit by it. They turned the corner and . . .

There it was, exactly as Vawn described it. A vast and wide cave, glowing with light, webbed with floating filaments that surged and swayed as if lifted by gentle breezes: veils of colour and light that crossed and crossed again, sometimes touching each other.

When they touched, the colours changed and the singing sounds swelled and great harmonies of pure thought gently entered the human minds.

'Vawn!' said the harmonies. 'Vawnnn . . . You always understood –'

'And now the others will,' Vawn said, her face lit by the shifting colours and her own smile. 'This is my mother, Sheila,' she said, suddenly sounding schoolgirlish and formal. 'And this is my father –'

'We know you all,' replied the voices. 'Your names, your souls, your minds –'

'But not our bodies,' Clyde said, 'Not our physical beings. You cannot know them. Can you?'

The voices laughed and said, 'Not your bodies. For we are bodiless. We are what you see. Nothing more –'

'And nothing less,' Jass said. His voice was hushed. 'You are – you are –' He would have said, 'wonderful', but the voices interrupted.

'We are just another part of the plan,' they sang.

'You called us murderers,' Makenzi said, jerking the words out. Like his father, he was stunned by the wonder of what he saw; but did not choose to yield too easily to the magic of the web.

'And so you were,' the voices replied, still with a tinge of amusement. 'But that is over now. You won your battles against the beasts. Won for yourselves and for us . . . Now you can be your true selves.'

'So the hunting is over?' said Tsu, her face soft in the ever-changing radiance of glowing colours.

'Over,' said the voices. 'Needless, now.'

'What part do we play now?' Ispex said gruffly. 'Now we've – restored the balance –'

'Yesss,' encouraged the voices. 'That is what you have done. Go on!'

'Well, now we've restored the balance, what next? There's still Tyrannopolis and the Octopus Emperor. Another fight to be fought –'

'Not now,' Jass said. 'Let's not think about that now.'

Ispex said, 'I suppose you're right. And we've got a new ally now, haven't we?'

'Usss!' said the voices of Moloch.

Ispex, still worried, said, 'But what happens next?'

'Roses, strawberries and wine,' the voices replied in a melody that somehow contained a joke.

And suddenly everyone was laughing and hugging each other; and the voices joined in the laughter, colouring it with gorgeous radiance and swaying, dancing filaments of mind.

* * *

Days later, aboard the shuttle . . .

'So we can take off and go back to Epsilon Cool,' Vawn said. 'I wonder how the other kittens have grown up? But of course, they won't be as lovely as Fang. Boofuls . . .' She nuzzled Fang and Ispex snorted.

'Sickening,' he said.

'You'll be sick yourself,' Tsu told him, 'if you go on hogging like that.'

'Why shouldn't I?' he replied. 'I like eating.'

'I like not having to hunt for the food,' Makenzi said. 'Don't you, Tsu?'

She did not reply. She licked an ice cream, without tasting it. Those hunting days . . . She licked her lips.

'When do we leave for home? – for Epsilon Cool?' Makenzi asked.

Shambles said, 'Any time. All necessary repairs to the shuttle have been complete-ete-ete-eted –'

'I must fix his stutter,' Tsu said, lazily. 'But first, can I have some more of this ice cream?'

'Who's being a pig now?' Ispex demanded, triumphantly.

Jass said, 'We can't take *Starstormer* with us, of course. And anyhow it's not fit to fly –'

'It is!' Ispex said, looking up. 'It's perfectly flightworthy! Everything checked and OK!' He was furious. 'We're not leaving old *Starstormer* here! Not on your life!'

'Not on *your* life!' Jass said, grimly. 'That thing was always a death-trap.'

'P-pardon!' Shambles said, agitatedly. 'I have checked everything – and in my opinion the ship is hardly –'

'Don't you dare say a word against *Starstormer*!' Vawn cried.

'Saved our bacon against the Octopus Emperor and Tyrannopolis, more than once,' Makenzi said, staring at his father. '*Your* bacon, too!'

Anxious to change the subject, Sheila said, 'Shambles, what's the Voice saying? The Voice of Tyrannopolis?'

'Oh, it's chuntering on,' Makenzi said, before the robot could reply. 'Usual stuff. Big threats. Nothing interesting. Look, about *Starstormer* –'

Dexter reached over and coded in Shambles's tape replay. There was the usual clutter of radio noise, then the Voice was heard.

'OBEY!' it snarled. 'Obey the Emperor! Do you seriously believe that Moloch will be your partner and ally? Are you really fools enough to believe that? How do you think Moloch, that cat's-cradle of bodiless brain, can help you fight the might of the Emperor? Learn to obey, *obey*, OBEY! Bow the knee to the Emperor! Bow –'

But then something went very wrong with Shambles' tapes, or perhaps it was his stutter. 'Bow!' said his speakers. 'Bow-wow-wow! Bow-wow-wow-wow!'

And all at once everyone was barking and woofing and Fang ran for cover and Makenzi, still barking furiously, stood on his head: and Tyrannopolis was just a mote of dust, light years away.

MORE EXCITING KNIGHT BOOKS FOR YOU TO ENJOY

STARSTORMERS

Nicholas Fisk

Makenzi, Vawn, Ispex and Tsu felt abandoned in their drab boarding school on Earth. How could they ever hope to join their parents, a thousand million miles away on Epsilon Cool? It was Makenzi who first said it (though Tsu pushed them into action) – *build* a spaceship! Together the children scoured the junkyards left over from the twentieth century and the result was *Starstormer*, a hollowed-out meteorite which, incredibly, proved spaceworthy. The Starstormers were launched on their first thrilling adventure . . .

KNIGHT BOOKS

SUNBURST

Nicholas Fisk

In their second adventure alone in Space, the Starstormers come across an immense abandoned spaceship, which appears to have come away from Earth. Its field signal reads *Plague ship! Keep away!* But it may contain vital equipment, so the four children decide to go aboard. Once there, they discover the ghost ship's hideous secret – *too late.* For now *Starstormer* cannot escape the other ship's gravity pull . . . and it is bound on a headlong course of self-destruction, destination – the sun!

KNIGHT BOOKS

CATFANG

Nicholas Fisk

Once again forced to leave Epsilon Cool to evade the evil Octopus Emperor, the Starstormers are beginning to feel that their escape-vehicle is now also a prison. *Starstormer* is showing dangerous signs of wear and tear, which adds to the strained atmosphere on board. As tension increases, distraction suddenly appears in the shape of a stowaway, a tousled, spiky, wet, filthy kitten. Cleaned up and given a name, 'Fang', he entertains the children with his antics. But not for long. *Starstormer* is once again under heavy attack – and Fang proves a surprising weapon, playing an amazing part in the great battle in Space!

KNIGHT BOOKS

THE BOY WHO SAVED EARTH

Jim Slater

It is the year 1985, and the Malagans – sinister, grey, jelly-like creatures – are mobilising their forces on Earth. Their strongest weapon is that no one even knows they are there . . . No one, that is except for Marcou – a boy from the highly advanced planet of Gundra – the sole survivor of a spaceship crash. He alone is able to locate and recognise the evil Malagans, but is there any way he can defeat them?

KNIGHT BOOKS

FRANKENSTEIN'S AUNT

Allan Rune Pettersson

'I'm going to put things straight in that castle again, even if werewolves and vampires are queuing up in the hall!'

Aunt Hanna Frankenstein is determined to restore her nephew's devastated castle to order and to clear the family's blackened name, but her bold words prove to be nearer the truth than she thought.

A hilariously spooky sequel to the famous Frankenstein story.

KNIGHT BOOKS

THE CASE OF THE FRIGHTENED ROCK STAR

Elizabeth Levy

With the help of her brother Jake, Jody Markson is organising a rock concert to raise money for the rebuilding of the school sports stadium. But a series of practical jokes, from red paint spilt over a batch of newly-printed posters to a mugging at the stadium, threatens to spoil all Jody's plans. Someone, somewhere, wants to discourage her – in a most sinister and menacing way.

What can be behind it all? With only a few days to the concert, Jody and Jake are determined to find out – and to expose the mysterious invisible joker.

The first Jody and Jake mystery.

KNIGHT BOOKS

THE CASE OF THE COUNTERFEIT RACEHORSE

Elizabeth Levy

Working at the local racecourse for the summer, Jody and Jake get the chance to live up to their reputation as amateur detectives. Jody is surprised when a nervous and unhealthy racehorse named Pure Energy makes an astonishing recovery after a very short stay at the vet's. Then a succession of 'accidents' result in her losing her job. When Pure Energy wins an unexpected victory and there are rumours of the race being fixed, Jody begins to suspect there's more to the horse's performance than meets the eye.

The second Jody and Jake mystery.

KNIGHT BOOKS

THE CASE OF THE FIRE-RAISING GANG

Elizabeth Levy

Cycling home from school one day, Jody and Jake witness a fire in a run-down district of Northtown. Arson is immediately suspected and Mark Brown, a teenage gang leader and pupil at Jody's school, is accused of the crime. Despite the evidence, Jody is convinced Mark is being framed, and she is determined to prove it.

Jody stumbles on the vital clue when someone sets fire to her bicycle – a sinister warning to stop investigating – and she realises the stakes are higher than she had at first thought possible . . .

The third Jody and Jake mystery.

KNIGHT BOOKS

KNIGHT BOOKS

☐	24878 5	STARSTORMERS	85p
☐	24879 3	SUNBURST	95p
☐	26529 9	CATFANG	95p
☐	26541 8	THE BOY WHO SAVED EARTH	95p
☐	28045 X	FRANKENSTEIN'S AUNT	£1.25
☐	28332 7	THE CASE OF THE FRIGHTENED ROCK STAR	95p
☐	28333 5	THE CASE OF THE COUNTERFEIT RACEHORSE	95p
☐	28585 0	THE CASE OF THE FIRE-RAISING GANG	95p

All these books are available at your local bookshop or newsagent, or can be ordered direct from the publisher. Just tick the titles you want and fill in the form below.

Prices and availability subject to change without notice.

KNIGHT BOOKS, P.O. Box 11, Falmouth, Cornwall.

Please send cheque or postal order, and allow the following for postage and packing:

U.K. – 45p for one book, plus 20p for the second book, and 14p for each additional book ordered up to a £1.63 maximum.

B.F.P.O. and EIRE – 45p for the first book, plus 20p for the second book, and 14p per copy for the next 7 books, 8p per book thereafter.

OTHER OVERSEAS CUSTOMERS – 75p for the first book, plus 21p per copy for each additional book.

Name ....

Address ....

....